OLD TIMES

ANCIENT ALMS-HOUSES OF ST. CROSS, WITH CURIOUS WOODEN ARCADE, ABINGDON.

OLD TIMES

RELICS, TALISMANS, FORGOTTEN CUSTOMS & BELIEFS OF THE PAST

BY

WALTER CLIFFORD MELLER

M.A., S.C.L.

ST. JOHN'S COLLEGE, OXFORD

Author of "A Knight's Life in the Days of Chivalry"

ILLUSTRATED

TOUCH-PIECE
(*The King's Healing*)

LONDON

T. WERNER LAURIE LIMITED

1925

Now Reissued by
Singing Tree Press
1249 Washington Blvd., Detroit, Michigan 1968

Library of Congress Catalog Card Number 68–26592

Manufactured in the United States of America
by Arno Press, Inc., New York

CONTENTS

LIST OF ILLUSTRATIONS

OLD TIMES

OLD BEDE-HOUSES AND HOSPITALS

THERE are certain old buildings in this country which, mellowed by age and clustered round like the ivy that embraces them with beautiful memories of medieval times, appeal not only to the antiquarian but to the kind-hearted in a very charming manner. We refer to the old bede-houses and hospitals found in so many English towns.

Here time seems to have stood still, and even in these noisy days peace seems to sit enthroned, and passing through some oak-studded door, champed with old hinges and cumbrous locks, or beneath some crumbling arch, we are brought back to another world when all that world was young.

Here, over these lichened stones, have countless feet in the past, of the sad, the homeless and the sick, passed. Here no one, if really deserving, has been refused a bed, a loaf and a shelter, and here daily prayers have gone forth for the pious founders and the lowly brethren. Alas! that in so many cases only a few stones are left of these sweet old bede-houses, and that now in their place the ugly poor-house is the only refuge for the homeless.

Passing by earlier references to hospitals, and closely connected with them, the alms or bede-houses, it is sufficient to quote the words of St.

Benedict in his Rule as to their institution: " Before all things and above all things special care must be taken of the sick, so that they may be served in very deed as Christ Himself, for He saith, ' I was sick and ye visited me,' and ' What ye did to one of these my least brethren ye did it to me.' "

This was the guiding thought, we might call it the coercion, which made our ancestors form these places, linked with the other, perhaps more selfish, conviction that in doing so they should obtain in the world beyond a recompense and expiation for the frailties of this life.

In the Rolls of Parliament (2 Henry V) we find the purpose of these places also stated very clearly: " Hospitals in cities, boroughs and divers other places to sustain blind men and women and people who have lost their goods and are fallen into great misfortune." One of the earliest of these ancient hospitals for relief was St. John's at Canterbury. Eadmer tells us in his day there were a hundred poor within it who could not, from age and infirmity, do any work, besides a hundred brothers and sisters in this alms-house, blind, lame, deaf and sick. The statutes of St. Mary's hospital at Chichester show us how such were received, and how on leaving God-speeded—" If any one in infirm health and destitute of friends should seek admission for a term until he shall recover, let him be gladly received and granted a bed. . . . In regard to the poor people who are received late at night and go forth early in the morning let the warden take care that their feet are washed, and as far as possible their necessities attended to."

In treating of the word "hospital" we must remember that the alms-house was a development of the original purpose of a hospital. To put it concisely—though there might be exceptions to this rule—the hospital was originally for transitory guests, whether hale or sick—the alms-house for permanent ones. Every monastery possessed the first—a guest-chamber or "hospitium," but unless certain persons had granted them "corrodies," by the conventual authorities or by the King's mandate, there were no permanent lodgers.

The description of St. Nicholas, Salisbury, shows this limited hospitality as against the permanent one of the alms-house—the inmates of the former are described as "passengers" (transcuntes). Again in the hospital, the inmates—unless it was a leper one—wore no distinctive marks, but those in the alms-house had clothing peculiar to the alms-house they inhabited. In hospitals the ever-changing crowd of poor who came and went and came again, lived while there under no rule, but those who lived for the rest of their lives in the alms-house always lived under certain rules defining their attendance at chapel and their devotions and deportment. Though primarily these alms-houses were for the aged it was not uncommon to find the young and strong side by side with its aged and infirm inmates. Several alms-houses maintained children. Bishop Grandison carried out his predecessor's (Stapledon's) intention of adding ten boys to the foundation of St. John's alms-house, Exeter, and Archbishop Chichele attached a boarding school to his bede-house at Higham Ferrers. In some cases, like St. Giles, Norwich, food was provided there for children who were getting their education elsewhere.

At St. Cross, Winchester, seven choristers were boarded and instructed, and thirteen poor boys from the Grammar School received there a substantial dinner a day.

If one asks what the bedesmen and women did in these picturesque houses, it may be briefly summed up—their life centred in their chapel; here they prayed for themselves, for the sick and for their founders' souls.

Nor were these chapels bare and unadorned. Lights were kept burning night and day before the altar. When on their patronal feast day the officials of the town came on a visit of inspection and worship, they were accustomed to leave many wax candles for the chapel to last during the year. At St. John's Hospital it was found a good way to provide such by fining any inmate in "wax candles" who reviled another inmate or used bad language in hall.

Books, plate and vestments the benefactors generally provided. Thus the founders of St. Giles, Norwich, bequeathed "the gilt cup which was the blessed St. Edmund's"; he also left a Bible to the House and a missal to the Master.

Even as late as the sixth year of Edward VI, St. John's, Canterbury, possessed vestments of black velvet, red velvet and white fustian and a cope of Bruges satin.

The original altar stones of three of these

bede-house chapels remain at Ripon, Stamford and Greatham.

In these chapels, the aged, the sick, if able, and destitute were continually to employ their time in prayer; so according to the Statutes of St. Mary's, Chichester, the brothers and sisters "must pray continually."

The alms-houses were built much on the same lines as the hospitals, but on a smaller scale. A good example exists at Higham Ferrers (1423). The hall was 63 feet; the chapel 17 feet. Wooden screens divided the dormitory, and the Statute there ordered each bedesman to join in evening prayer at his chamber door. The chapel was nearly always under the roof of the alms-house—sometimes the roof lowered where it was situated, sometimes raised higher than the secular part of the house; only one example has been found of the great hall of a bede-house having a detached chapel—that at St. John's, Northampton.

We can also, in the alms-house or hospital at St. Cross, Winchester, see one built in a statelier manner. Here the refectory adjoins the tower, on the west side; it is distinguished from the domestic buildings beyond by its bold porch and flight of steps, and by three perpendicular transomed windows. Internally it conveys a good idea of a hall in one of the older and larger bede-houses. It is 43 feet long, 24 feet in breadth and 32 feet in height to the apex of the rafters. An open hearth occupies the centre of the chamber, and round the glowing embers of this central fire the

Brethren of to-day still quaff their ale and sing their songs on Gaudy days. The Minstrels Gallery remains over the entrance screen:

" Merry it is in halle to heare the harps,
The minstrelles synge, the jonglours carpe."

But the chief feature is the fine open-timbered roof. The original stained glass is still in the upper lights and depicts the Royal Arms and the hat of Cardinal Beaufort with the surrounding motto: "A honor et lyesse." Remembering the close affinity in architecture and its artists that in the Middle Ages this country had with France, it is more than a surmise that some of the old hospitals in the latter country show us what were similarly constructed in England. There the commonest form seems to have been a great hall divided by pillars into a centre and aisles in which rows of beds were arranged, with a chapel in a square building at the end of the hall, and other buildings irregularly disposed in a courtyard as in the Hôtel Dieu of Chartres, built in 1153, and the Salle des Morts at Ourscamp. At Tartoine, near Laon la Fère, the hospitium is on a different form than these. It consists of a hall with cells on one side of it, and is placed on one side of a square courtyard, and the chapel and lodgings for the Brothers on another side of the court.

Very much like the arrangement of these French hospitals was that of St. Bartholomew's, London. It consisted of a double hall, or a single hall with aisles. Between the aisles or at the end of the hall was the chapel. In either aisle were the beds of the sick, the men on one side, the women on the other. As the patients were brought in they were put to bed—two, four, even eight in one bed, without any regard to the form of disease they might be suffering from, or the danger of infection to the others. The chaplain was always in attendance to smooth the path of the dying and give the last Sacraments; while far from the patients grumbling at their beds, or the draughts in the great hall, the hospital seemed a paradise to them after the hovels they were brought from. The remedies applied to them by the doctor—who always in those days, if clever, was an ecclesiastic—were of the simplest sort, remedies grounded on old wives' lore of herbs and simples.

DRESS

The early type of a pensioner's gown worn in all alms-houses is perpetuated at St. Cross. At Croydon the founder provided gowns of dark and brown colour. At Ewelme the bedesman had a brighter one—" a tabard of his own, with a red cross on the breast and a hood." At Alkmonton a suit every third year alternately white and russet. Two of the servitors at St. Nicholas, Pontefract, wore a livery called "White Livery." Before admittance to a bede-house, anciently, a short service was held, after which the man or woman about to be admitted cast off their former apparel and clothed themselves in the bede-house livery. Each also took a sort of oath on entering. Thus at St. Nicholas he or she promised to keep the peace, to do their " devoir " so that every brother and sister should also be in peace, and also in love and charity with each other: to show this pleasant wish the newly admitted gave their right hands in fellowship to the other brothers and sisters.

All these charitable institutions were under a definite rule, either that of the diocesan bishop or of the monastic order with which they were in touch. Bishop Poore of Sarum (1223) in his " Constitutions " headed one clause: " Concerning the Rule of Religion, and in what manner it is lawful to found a Xenolochium." Some lay founders, therefore, had to apply direct for an episcopal constitution; others applied the rules, with modifications, of the monastic house their newly-built alms-house would be in touch with; but all appointments to the offices in such were in the patrons' hands, and both their officials and the bedesmen were admitted by a religious ceremony.

These rules to admit none without examination were necessary, particularly after the " Black Death " which had ravaged the whole country and disorganized the ancient practices obtaining in the feudal manors. Those who had laboured on such had died in such numbers that the remaining ones, who had been tied to the soil, and prevented offering their services elsewhere than to the lord of their own manor, broke these contracts, and, where they did not get work, wandered about the country as vagrants.

What was worse and would inevitably happen was, that many among them, not being able, or not willing, to work, took up begging or robbing by profession.

These " wandering labourers became mere beggars in order to lead an idle life and betake themselves out of their own districts to the cities, boroughs, and other good towns to beg, and they are able-bodied and might well ease the community if they would serve." (Rolls of Parchment, II, p. 340, A.D. 1376.)

We can see from this how careful and necessary it was that the wardens and masters of these medieval alms-houses had to be before they admitted the starving poor to the benefit of their houses. Only the deserving—and these after a service of a sacred character—could participate in such. Even if such came with seeming devotion on their lips, a particular scrutiny was necessary, for as the Rolls of Parliament disclose, such vagrants who had escaped from their lord's manor would often profess religion, and assert that their wandering was that of pilgrimage, while they even forged " false letters of credit " to establish this falsehood.

It is no wonder that such places as Coventry, Canterbury and London, with their bede-houses, had great attractions for such vagrants, and that a very zealous inquiry had to be made before any but " godly and deserving poor " were admitted to these refuges; and that if some of these stalwart vagrants failed to get into these religious houses, they haunted the ale-houses and inns. There is a curious epitome in Langland's " Piers Plowman " of the mixed company in these ale-houses, which, if they could by hook or crook gain admittance to, all these " broken men " and vagrants frequented in the fourteenth century.

B

" Thomme the tynkere and tweye of hus knaues
Hicke the hakeneyman, and Houwe the neldere (needle-
    seller)
Claryce of Cockeslane, the clerk of the Churche
Syre Peeres of Prydie, and Purnel of Flaundres,
An haywarde and an heremyte, the hangeman of Tyborne
Dauwe the dykere, with a dosen harlotes
Of portours and of pykeporses, and pylede toth-drawers."

And Christine de Pisan shows us these fighting and
drinking in such an inn—

> " Par ces trouveriez a sejour
> Aussi tost que ont fait leur journee.
> Maint y aconvient aler boire :
> La despendent, c'est chose voire,
> Plus que toute jour n'ont gaigne.
> .   .   .   .   .
> La ne convient il demander
> S'ilz s'entrebatent quand sont yvres :
> Le prevost en a plusieurs livres
> D'amande tout au long de l'an."

As late as the year 1538 the citizens of London in
petitioning Henry VIII to re-found certain of these
bede-houses and hospitals, after praying all impotent
persons not able to labour shall be relieved, conscious
of the frauds of these vagrants in the past, on these
charitable refuges of the worthy poor, added: " and
all sturdy beggars not willing to labour shall be
punished so that with God's grace few or no persons
shall be seen abroad to beg or ask ' almesse.' "

However, the warden and his officials of the
alms-houses, if rule and regulation could serve, took
good care to enforce such rules on the bedesmen.
We have seen how their days were measured out by
prayer in these chapels, and if they went outside their

gates, regulations also followed them. At Croydon, for instance, they were forbidden to walk or gaze in the streets, nor might they go out of sight of home, excepting to church.

By the rules of St. Katherine's alms-house, Rochester, they were to be continuously engaged in work that " the devil may not find them with nothing to do."

Again, if the bedesmen bought ale, it was to be consumed at home, that none either outside be quarrelsome or a debater; that none of them haunt a tavern.

At St. Mary's, Chichester, the regulations were very drastic, and no doubt were likewise the same in other houses. "If a brother shall have a quarrel with a brother with noise and riot, then let him fast for seven days on Wednesdays and Fridays on bread and water and sit at the bottom of the table and without a napkin. If a brother shall be found to have money or property concealed from the warden let the money be hung round his neck and let him be well flogged and do penance for thirty days, as before." At Sherburn the prior was not to spare the rod. Chastisement was to be well meted out to the idle and refractory, and if such objected to a whipping, he was to be put on bread and water.

It will be seen from all this our forefathers were wise men and very much alive to the evils of promiscuous charity and idleness, and that though they erected all through the land religious refuges and hospitals their hands fell heavily on vagrants and those who refused to be under rule and objected to

work.   If the Church thus felt, so also did the State.
Anyone reading the many statutes passed in the reign
of Edward III and Richard II can verify this fact.
It is a lesson our own age might well take to heart.
If with open hands Charity received in the Middle
Ages the poor and destitute, she expected an obedient
return from such, in prayer, in work, and submission.

We have dealt principally above with the alms-
houses, either those severed from the monasteries or
founded by those institutions with the same view in
end—to house the old, the feeble and destitute, but
it would not be treating of the subject properly if some
account was not also given of the houses called
" lazar-houses," particularly as several of these—this
fell disease as time went on becoming rare in England
—became afterwards simply alms-houses for the old
and destitute.   At what time leprosy gained its great
hold in England is not known.   Some trace its origin
from Egypt during the tenth century, others state it
was introduced here by the returning Crusaders,
notwithstanding that Syria was singularly free from
the scourge at the time of the Crusades.   Whatever
its origin, there is no doubt that the disease was very
rife in this country for many years, probably some
years before the first Crusade, for the known existence
of leper-hospitals and lazar-houses, like St. Nicholas
Hospital, Harbledown, founded ten years before the
first Crusade, are proofs that the Crusaders did not
first introduce it here.   In Saxon times leprosy is not
mentioned in any co-eval document.   In 1217-28, we

find it appearing in the "Ancran Riewle" of Richard Poore, Bishop of Salisbury.

Leprosy, too, was not confined to the poorer classes—all ranks it attacked. Thus we find the son of Petronelle, heiress of the great Anglo-Norman House of Grantmesnil and married to Robert Blanchesmains (1173-8), a victim. Knighton, the old chronicler, says she built the nave of the Abbey Church at Leicester and caused a rope to be made out of her own hair to suspend a lamp in the choir. William the leper, her son, founded the hospital of St. Leonard at Leicester for brother lepers. He also is credited with building another there dedicated to St. Edmund. This latter became an alms or bede-house.

At first these afflicted people were nursed in the monastic infirmaries, but gradually, realizing the terrible disease and danger of contamination, they were removed to isolated hospitals of their own. The great majority of these refuges were founded between 1084 and 1224. Over such the master himself might be a leper. Thus an injunction of 1223 showed that at St. Leonard's, Lancaster, it was customary for the lepers to elect one of themselves as master. In 1342 the Prior of St. Bartholomew's, Rochester, was a leper. At Dover, the regulations allowed the master might be a leper. The priests serving lepers in their chapels were permitted to dispense rites which did not pertain usually to the unbeneficed clergy, i.e., to hear their confessions, to absolve, to administer the Eucharist and Extreme Unction, yet such were difficult to find, for often they themselves became lepers, and few would brave that danger as did St. Hugh and, after centuries, Father Damien.

No better view can be obtained of the seclusion and isolation these poor lepers had to endure, whether permitted outside their houses, or within, than that given in the office at the " Seclusion of a leper " according to the Use of Sarum. We here abbreviate and give some of its salient points.

First of all the sick man, or the leper, clad in a cloak and in his usual dress, being in his house, ought to have notice of the coming of the priest who is on his way to lead him to the church, and must in that guise wait for him. For the priest, vested in a surplice and stole, with the Cross going before, makes his way to the leper's house. . . . He exhorts him to patience, and cheers him that if he bears his afflictions rightly he will reach a better home, that of eternal felicity. He sprinkles him with holy water. On coming to the church the leper is to be placed beneath a black cloth after the manner of a dead man. There on his knees beneath it he is to hear Mass; afterwards he is to be taken to a certain spot outside, where, again sprinkled with holy water, the priest addresses him with words of divine consolation, and leading him again to his house chants certain Introits and Collects suitable to the occasion for the poor man's state. Then when they arrive into the open fields the priest imposes on him these prohibitions:

(1) I forbid you ever to enter churches, or to go into a market, or a mill, or a bake-house, or into any assemblies of people.

(2) Also I forbid you ever to wash your hands or even any of your belongings in stream or spring of water of any kind, and if you are thirsty you must drink water from your cup or some other vessel.

(3) Also I forbid you ever henceforth to go out without your leper's dress that you may be recognized by others, and you must not go outside your house door unshod.

(4) Also I forbid you wherever you may be to touch anything you may wish to buy otherwise than with a rod or staff to show what you want.

(5) Also I forbid you ever henceforth to enter taverns or other houses if you wish to buy wine, and take care even what they give you they put into your cup.

(6) Also I forbid you to have any intercourse with any woman except your own wife.

(7) Also I command you when you are on a journey not to return an answer to anyone who questions you till you have gone off the road leeward, so that he may take no harm from you; and that you never go through a narrow lane lest you should meet someone.

(8) Also I charge you if need require you to pass over some toll-way through rough ground or elsewhere, that you touch no posts or things whereby you cross, till you have first put on your gloves.

(9) Also I forbid you to touch infants or young

folk whosoever they may be, or to give to them or to others any of your possessions.

(10) Also I forbid you henceforth to eat or drink in any company except that of lepers. And know that when you die you will be buried in your own house unless it be by favour obtained beforehand in the Church.

Then this note is added: That before the leper enters his house he ought to have a coat and shoes of fur, under plain shoes, and his leper-signal, the clapper, a hood and a cloak, two pairs of sheets, a cup, a funnel, a girdle, a small knife and a plate. His house ought to be small, with a well, a couch furnished with coverlets, a pillow, a chest, a table, a seat, a candlestick, a shovel, a pot, and other useful articles.

When all is complete the priest is to remind him of the ten rules he has heard and been pledged to. Next he is to be reminded of the ten commandments of God, and that every day as a Christian he is bound to say a Paternoster, Ave Maria, Credo in Deum and Credo in Spiritum. When the priest leaves him he says: " Worship God and give thanks to God. Have patience and the Lord be with thee. Amen."

This form of " entombment " was used when the leper was isolated in his own house. It reads almost like people thus closed up in their dwellings centuries after in the time of the Great Plague; only in the leper's case, even under these iron-bound restrictions, he was permitted to go out. As time went on and money was available, hospitals for the leprous became more usual, where, herded together and under care of a warden or master, a chaplain and a doctor, who in those days was an ecclesiastic, they were supervised and treated. Less and less, therefore, with their clappers or their bell warding off the healthy, were they found on the wide heaths or broken roads of the country. Secluded in these hospitals, under rule, they often broke out in revolt. Their very infirmities caused them to become irritable and abusive. Officials therefore were accustomed to visit the lazar-houses daily to chastise such and even to use corporal punishment. To keep an eye on his refractory household, the warden was never to be absent at night, nor for long by day, although he was allowed for recreation to walk a mile or two at certain times.

One thing we find strange in some of these leper-houses—the endeavour of those who were untouched by the scourge and really healthy, trying sometimes to get into these hospitals and participate in what the house offered in board and bed. In 1164 Pope Alexander III forbade the officials of St. James's Lazar-house at Thanington to admit into the sister-hood of lazars any who were not infected, because healthy women were constantly begging admission. The lazar-house of St. Bartholomew's, Oxford, in 1321 was stated to be full of healthy and sturdy men. All this we think shows, even with the bede-houses and hospitals and lazar-houses available, how inadequate they were to stem the vast number of homeless men and women, whether hale or sick, in the

Middle Ages, and particularly after the " Black Death."

After many years, when the dread disease of leprosy waned and at last was virtually stamped out in England, many of these hospitals, devoted to such, lapsed into bede or alms-houses and remain such to this day. Perhaps one of the most curious examples is the transformation of a lazar-hospital into a palace, where St. James's, London, now stands.

If it be asked how all these houses obtained funds, such were drawn from: (1) Grants by the original founders from land and monies. (2) From endowments in kind—these chiefly from the king, such as wood for fuel from his forests, also herbage for the hospital's sheep, etc. (3) From bequests—Henry II left large sums to such houses both in England and Normandy, particularly for lepers. Nobles and citizens followed his example. Thus, when in 1174 Henry II went on pilgrimage to Canterbury to do penance at Becket's shrine he stopped at Harbledown, entered the little church still standing, where he confessed and was absolved, and for the love of St. Thomas he gave twenty marks of rent to the leper-house.

The original from manuscript in the British Museum runs:

> " Juste Cantorbire unt lepros un hospital
> U mult ad malades de gent plein mal :
> Près une liwe i ad del mustier principal
> Là ù li cors saint gist del mire espirital
> Ki manit dolent ad mis en joie e en estal

Dunc descendi iluec li reis à Herebaldun
E entra el mustier, e a fet sa oreison
De trestuz ses mesfez ad requis Deu pardun
Pur amur saint Thomas a otrie eu dun
Vint marchies de rentes à la povre maison."

It was at this leper-house in Harbledown, King John of France, while captive in England, made a second, and at this lazar-house, formally founded by Lanfranc, donated "ten gold crowns" *pour les nonnais de Harbledown.* Sometimes Harbledown was called " Bob up and down " from its uneven ground around, and so Chaucer refers to it as such:

" Wist ye not where standeth a little town
Which that yclept is Bob-up-and-down
Under the Blee in Canterbury way."

It was a great advantage to their funds if any of these leper-houses possessed a relic and also were on the pilgrims' way to Canterbury. Both these qualifications Harbledown possessed. The relic was the shoe of St. Thomas à Becket. Probably it was for paying his orisons before this relic Edward, the Black Prince, stopped there and left alms for the lepers on his way to Canterbury. (4) From holding fairs. Such was one among others near Cambridge, where the proceeds of tolls and booths went to the leper-house. (5) From voluntary contributions. These often were received during divine service in Church; sometimes by a brother of the house going through the country-side asking for alms.

Many Royal letters licensed such to be collected in the churches, towns, fairs and markets for these poor or afflicted ones. Bishops, too, were not behind the sovereign in this. They issued briefs on behalf of these houses of charity in their own or dioceses beyond. From all these sources and others these institutions for the leper, the sick, the homeless and those past work, derived their funds.

These houses were scattered so profusely about the country that the last edition of the " Monasticon " enumerates no less than three hundred and seventy of them. Those (not lazar ones) but alms-houses for the old and poor, had usually a little chamber for each person, a common hall in which they took their meals, a chapel in which divine service was held.

One of the most beautiful of these, and still existing, is that of Ewelme, Oxfordshire, built of the mellowed fifteenth century bricks, as beautiful and structurally sound as the pious founders left it. These were the unhappy William de la Pole, first Duke of Suffolk, and his good wife, Duchess Alice, granddaughter of the poet Chaucer. He was the favourite minister of Henry VI, was exiled by the Yorkist faction, and beheaded by sailors on his way to banishment. Twenty-five years of widowhood fell to the bereaved duchess, who finished her husband's buildings, the church, manor house, school and the alms-houses, which she called " God's House," and then rested beneath one of the finest monuments in England in the church hard by.

Even after the dissolution of the monasteries and in Reformation times, many of these quaint and beautiful bede-houses were erected.

Many city merchants of London, having made their fortunes, remembered the little villages that gave them birth, whence they had gone as poor boys to seek for wealth, and built alms-houses therein, placing them in charge of their city company. Thus in many villages or small towns we find these pleasant buildings. Such is the charming Carolean Lucas's Hospital in Wokingham, founded by Henry Lucas in 1663, and managed by the Drapers' Company, and the Jesus Hospital at Bray, founded by William Goddard in 1610, and controlled by the Fishmongers, for " forty poor people to dwell in and inhabit."

We have seen the older hospitals were often called bede-houses; it was because the inmates were bound to pray for their founders and benefactors, and because their chief occupation was to be prayer. And " bede," we know, is the old Saxon word for prayer. How different to the modern workhouse! Just as is to-day how different from those good old times of England.

" When her gentleman had hands to give, and her yeomen
        hearts to feel,
    And they raised up many a bede-house, but never a
        bastille;
    And the poor they honoured, for they knew that He
        who for us bled
    Had seldom, when He came on earth to lay His Head."

Examples also of the architecture of these ancient bede-houses may be seen in the bede-houses in Higham Ferrers churchyard built by Archbishop Chichele in 1422; St. Thomas's Hospital, Northampton; Wyston's Hospital, Leicester; Ford's Hospital, Coventry; the Alms-houses, Sherborne; the Leicester Hospital, Warwick.

Many of the beautiful old bede-houses existing in London, particularly at Westminster, are destroyed, and with them have perished the sentiment and the romance of the streets of our great city. Something still remains, for with the most laudable desire to destroy whatever can teach or suggest or soften manners or point to heaven, the Charity Commissioners have left at Westminster one or two ancient schools, notably the " Grey Coat." The great hall where the almsmen once lived is now the school hall, the old dormitory is now thrown open to the roof, but still at the back are the wide gardens.

There were two alms-houses in the Woolstaple (now Cannon Street). They looked out on the river, and the bedesmen, in later times, turned a penny by letting rooms in them to Parliament-men.

There were other alms-houses founded by Henry VII outside the Gate-house, Tothill Street. There was another founded by his mother, Lady Margaret, in the Almonry. All these, like many other valuable relics of the past, have disappeared.

QUEEN ELEANOR'S CROSS, NORTHAMPTON.

THE OLD STONE CROSSES OF BRITAIN

Tertullian (" De Corona Militis "), writing A.D. 196, says of the frequency the early Christians used the Cross, at " every commencement of business, whenever we go in or come out of any place, when we dress for a journey, when we go into a bath, when we go to meat, when lights are brought in, when we lie down or sit down and whatever business we have we make on our foreheads the sign of the Cross."

And another writer later, St. Chrysostom, in 350, goes further and gives valuable evidence of crosses erected in places. " In the private houses," he says, " in the public market-places, in the desert, on the highway, on mountains, on hills, on the sea, on ships, on islands are crosses."

If in those early ages such was the case, it is little wonder that throughout Christendom the erection of crosses obtained freely. Indeed, they had imperial sanction, for the Emperor Constantine in 324-37 caused by Edict such to be erected along the public highways where in pagan times had stood statues of the gods defining different territories and properties. At the time of the Reformation, in England alone, it has been reckoned roughly there were five thousand crosses.

Before more particularly entering into their different purposes and appearances it may be pointed out that when Christianity obtained, many of the

31

menhirs, monoliths and stones formerly used for
pagan worship were, by incising their surface with a
cross, dedicated to Christian use.

This practice obtained also for wells, previously
pagan.

Even many churches were erected on the foundation of old temples, the latter themselves consecrated
to Christian worship.

The origin of Stone (monumental) Crosses in this
country of the Anglo-Saxon period must, however, be
traced back to an even earlier, that of the Celtic and
preceding one.   These rough unhewn obelisks were
erected to commemorate chieftains—probably such
as were slain in battle, and the value of the
tribute to their memory lay in the great size of
the stone and the consequent difficulty in raising
it.   After the introduction of Christianity the
Symbol of the Cross was often on these placed
enclosed in a circle—the emblem of Eternity.   From
these rude and Christian monuments developed the
graceful and elaborate ornamental crosses of a later
period.

The crosses at Penrith are a good example of
these pillar-stones, very little differing in outline from
the pagan monoliths.

These earliest crosses may be divided into two
classes—first, the Pillar Crosses just mentioned;
secondly, the Interlaced Crosses, which are rude
stones carved into the shape of a cross erected upon
a base, with more or less ornament of interlaced bands
or cords graven on them.   On them often engraved in

either Latin, Celtic or Norse or in the Runic letters
of Northern Europe—inscriptions such as " A. erected
this Cross to the memory of B. Pray for his soul."
These crosses are found at a hundred and eighty
different localities in Great Britain. On some are
found, besides religious figures, hunting scenes,
representations of warriors and huntsmen on horseback, together with stags and hounds. These are
most frequently found in Scotland, and some in
Ireland; when in the latter country these representations occur most frequently upon the base rather than
the shaft of the cross.

It has been thought by some these hunting
pictures have a mystic Christian significance—as the
chase of a man's soul by the evil spirits is often
referred to by early writers. Sometimes on these
rude crosses, as has been said, inscriptions are found.
At Beckermet (in Northumberland) one such bears
this inscription as translated:

> " Here enclosed
> Tuda Bishop;
> The plague destruction before,
> The reward of Paradise after."
> —" Runic Monuments," I, 390, note.

Again another, with doubtful translation:

> " Here beacons
> Two set up
> Queen Arlec
> For her son Athfeshar
> Pray for our
> Souls."

C

It is no doubt from this circumstance, i.e., using stone menhirs and dedicating such to Christian art, that as regards Britain, particularly in Cornwall and in the northern kingdom of the west of Scotland, stone crosses and seldom wood were found.   The weather, too, of our isles, often stormy and tempestuous, unlike the sun-dried fields of Southern Europe, dictated to the rearer of a cross to fashion it of stone, while in the drier atmosphere of Southern Italy and France, the crosses, as to-day, are most frequently of wood.

However, even in our own country some were made of wood.   Thus Joan Wither bequeathed a sum in 1511 for the restoration of the wooden cross in the village of Reding, Kent.   Again, John Nethesway of Taunton, Somerset, whose will is dated August, 1503, directed his executors to " make a new crosse of tree in the churchyard of St. Mary Magdalyn nigh the procession way "—i.e., the outdoor processions, particularly at Ascensiontide, which the medieval Church was in the habit of making.

Now in the remains of crosses still found in this country, it will be obvious to one searching for them, that there is the inequality of their distribution.   Some counties, as Somerset, Gloucestershire, contain numbers, while others hardly any.   Yet it would be wrong to conclude from this they never existed.   In Kent, for instance, with the exception of two ancient crosses in Folkestone and in Teynham, there is not one other example extant.   Yet numbers and numbers of Kentish Churchyard Crosses are positively known, through mention of them in old wills, to have been standing in the Middle Ages.

The reason for some counties preserving some and some almost denuded, is probably where the officials of the Reformation, bent on their destruction, were most zealous, or where the Cromwellian bigots of his armies were most industrious, or the monastic bodies had so (as at Abingdon) long infuriated their tenants that they destroyed at their suppression everything reminding them of their servitude.

The plinths or shafts of most of these crosses, when those crosses were thus simple and not Market Crosses or Preaching Crosses, far, in size, outweighed the Cross proper they held up—nor did they all bear on the Cross the Figure of the Crucified. When they did so, as a rule, the Figure was draped. It was, in fact, always so in early medieval figures, while the face was portrayed as beardless and in the flower of youth, till the Black Death and the expectation of an early coming of the Day of Judgment led the later artists to carve the Figure naked, bearded, and as the Man of Sorrows. Indeed there are only two known representations of the Redeemer in relief (the most were incised) on the Cross previous to the ninth century, and, as before said, in the earliest types Christ appears as the King reigning from the Tree, His Head erect, regally crowned, His Body vested in an alb. At Kilmartin, in Argyllshire, is one of the two representations known where the Figure is undraped, His Head bent sorrowfully, without crown or halo, short-haired and beardless. On the other side of this wonderful

cross-shaft there are faintly discernible traces where
the Figure is fully draped, His Hands raised in
blessing, while the position of the Feet suggest a
seated Figure.

Sometimes the shaft of the crosses was extremely
high, while, as we said, the cross itself is extremely
small. To take another instance from Scotland, in
Iona is one called Maclean's Cross, it stands twenty
feet high, yet the Crucifixion is small within a circle.

The most ancient example of sculpture (i.e., for
a crucifix) from the nude living model to be found in
medieval England, was at the Abbey of Meaux, near
Beverley, where the Abbot records, " The artist of this
never worked at any fine or important part of it except
on Fridays, fasting on bread and water, and he had all
the time a naked man under his eyes, and he laboured
to give to his crucifix the beauty of the model."

Another point may be touched on. In Britain,
both in England and Scotland, differing in this from
the past and present day practice abroad, where crosses
are found often isolated along the roads, ours seem
nearly always to have been placed in, or close to,
towns, abbeys and churches. Even in the case of the
famed Eleanor Crosses, such were erected in the
towns, not along the roads proper her bier was carried.

It may be well to enumerate now, how these ancient
crosses have been divided. They seem to have
been:

(1) Memorial. (2) Market Crosses. (3) Preaching Crosses. (4) Weeping Crosses. (5) Boundary
or Sanctuary Crosses.

(1) As to Memorial, the most celebrated of such are the Eleanor Crosses, which will be touched on a little later.

(2) The Market Crosses originated in towns where there were monastic establishments. They formed a central point where the monks collected the tolls and tithes due from their farmers and flocks. The original form of these so-called crosses was simply a cross like the old one which was at Chester, but as time passed, to shelter the ecclesiastic collecting the abbey rents and taxes, a covering over it was added, as in the Cheddar Cross in Somerset. From these small covered crosses again, after a time, developed those we see still in many country towns, and which, like the one at Shrewsbury, affords covered space under it for a hundred people with the produce they bring to sell. In all these Market Crosses the religious and early reason for crosses seems to have merged into a purely materialistic one. Some of the crosses, as at Gloucester, Coventry and Abingdon, had little turrets, with vanes, called girouettes, because they revolved with the wind and, being gilt, glittered in the sun.

(3) A third division we may place crosses in, are the so-called Preaching Crosses. These, even in their scanty remains, are very interesting. These crosses were used chiefly by the mendicant orders— the Franciscan or the Dominicans. Both orders came into this country to preach the Gospel to the poor. The Cistercians also had the same object, at their first introduction into this country. They kept ascetic

rules, and carried about the highways and towns
"preaching stools" on which they addressed their
audiences. From these movable preaching stools
came the Preaching Crosses as a more convenient and
dignified—though not so portable—way of addressing
the rustics and townsfolk. One of the most celebrated
of these was Paul's Cross in London. Here in 1461
the Bishop of Exeter preached, urging the better title
of the House of York. Here Dr. Shaw, a little later,
preached against the validity of the young Prince
Edward V's title to the crown. Later, in state,
Charles I went to hear Laud preaching.

There is such a Preaching Cross still at Iron Acton.
The ceiling within the cross is vaulted, the upper
part elaborately carved with angels and coats of arms.
This cross dates from about 1410-20.

One of the most celebrated of these Preaching
Crosses is the Black Friars Cross at Hereford, which
probably dates from the time of Richard II. It is
hexagonal in plan and is mounted on steps. In the
majority of cases, a learned writer on the subject states,
it is likely that there was not in most cases a distinctive
Pulpit Cross, the steps of the ordinary Churchyard
Cross thus serving. There remain now no more than
two crosses obviously and primarily designed as
"Preaching Crosses," viz., the two already mentioned
—that of Iron Acton in Gloucestershire, and that of
the Black Friars Cross at Hereford.

It was at these convenient Preaching Crosses,
being chiefly the place for the mendicant friars' use,
that the worldly minded of them stood like pedlars

and sold to the country-people their little goods.   The old song of such says:

" Thai wandren here and there
  And dele with dyvers marcerye
  Right as thai pedlers were
  Thai dele with purses, pynnes and knyves,
  With girdles, gloves, for wenches and wyves."

(4) A fourth division crosses have been divided into are those called " Weeping Crosses." Antiquarians are much perplexed to give a reason for such, and also the name given to this division—yet remembering the time these crosses were erected—a time when penances were entailed on those having sinned, their name and calling seems obvious.   The confessor would, as a penance, say to one who had confessed his or her sins—" as a penance go to such and such a cross and there weep over your delinquencies and bemoan your state," and to these crosses perhaps direct the penitent to go barefoot. Hence the cross became named a " Weeping Cross."

The memory of Weeping Crosses is preserved in the old English proverb, " The way to Heaven is by Weeping Cross."   Another old saying was, " He that goeth out with often loss, At last comes home by Weeping Cross."   A noted " Weeping Cross " was used, however, not always for penitential observances. At Shrewsbury, such, on the Feast of Corpus Christi, was visited by various gilds to offer prayers for a good harvest.   Sometimes, too, such crosses, fitly called then "weeping " as a mark of private grief, were set up.   Thus at Caen such was raised in memory of the tears and sorrows that Matilda, queen of William the Conqueror, had endured owing to his cruelties.

Again it has been suggested why suicides were buried at cross-roads was, because the Boundary or Weeping Cross was often there so that those passing by it might be moved to pray for the suicide, unburied in consecrated ground, on seeing this Cross of Weeping Penitence.

Such are the four divisions given to our ancient crosses, but the first division, those called " Memorial," should be here briefly touched on again, for it would be a great omission not to refer particularly to those beautiful Memorial Crosses called " Eleanor Crosses."

Their erection arose, as we know, from the pathetic love of Edward I for his wife. A stone cross was built along the route her body was carried—not the most direct route, but arranged that her body might rest each night at some large or important town or else at some convent for the fitting celebration of the solemn offices for the dead. These stations, where afterwards crosses were erected, were at Lincoln, Grantham, Stamford, Geddington, Northampton, Dunstable, St. Albans, Waltham and London—at the latter the body probably lay for the night in St. Paul's and afterwards was conveyed to the village of Charing, the last resting-place before entombment at the Abbey.

Here, it may be said, the queen's heart was deposited in the Church of the Preaching Friars, and the bowels in the Chapel of the Virgin in Lincoln Minster, where there is also a statue to her, and another to her husband, of singular beauty and dignity.

Alas! all these beautiful crosses have disappeared except those of Geddington, Northampton, and Waltham—these three are fortunately in a good state of preservation.

Their variety of design suggest they were not all the work of the same hand.

That at Geddington is unlike any English Gothic architecture, and has much the appearance of the art of Spain. Possibly one of the queen's own countrymen did the work.

Geddington now is a small village, but, in those days, it possessed a royal palace, where often weighty affairs in the State were deliberated. It was here Henry II decided on his expedition to the Holy Land.

The three crosses left show how graceful and beautiful must have been the others—almost fairy-like in their graceful tapering Gothic.

Whether the one at Charing Cross gave the name to that locality " Chere-reine " is doubtful. It is pleasant to think it did, but it seems far more likely the name of the place previously was " Charing." A curious dialogue written by a certain Henry Peacham between the Crosses of Charing and Cheape describes them " as fearing their fall in these uncertain tymes " —which indeed two years after happened.

Charing Cross is made to say, " I am all of white marble, which is not perceived of every one, and so cemented of the purest lime. In Henry VIII's time I was begged and should have been degraded for that

I had—then in Edward the Sixe, when Somerset House was building, I was in danger; after that in the reign of Queen Elizabeth one of her footmen had like to run away with me, but the greatest danger of all I was in, when I quaked with fear, was in the reign of King James, for then I was eight times begged of him, part of me to make a kitchen chimney for a constable at Shoreditch—an innkeeper bargained for as much of me as would make two troughs, one to water his guests' horses, the other to give his swine their meat. The rest of my poore carcase should hence been carried I know not whither, to the repaire of a decayed old stone bridge (as I am told) on the top of Harrow Hill."

Cheapside Cross is made to say this: "After this most valuable and excellent king had built me in forme, answerable in beauty and proportion to the rest, I fell to decay, at which time John Hatherly, Mayor of London, having first obtained a licence of King Henry VI, 1441, I was repaired in a beautiful manner. John Fisher, a mercer, after that gave 600 marks to my new erecting a building. In the second year of King Henry VII I was gilded over against the arriving in of Charles V, Emperor, and again newly gilded against the coronation of King Edward VI, and gilded again against the coronation of King Philip. Lord! how often have I been 'presented' by juries of the quest, for incumbrance of the street, yet I have kept my standing. I shall never forget how upon the 21st of June, 1581, my lower statues were pulled down in the night and sent down, e.g., the Resurrection of Christ, the image of the Virgin Mary, Edward the Confessor and the rest. The Queen (Elizabeth) sent a strict command (thereupon) that Sir William Ryder, Lord Mayor, ' should respect my antiquity.' "

Alas! poor Crosses. The Commonwealth spared neither of you. The statue where King Charles looks down Whitehall is the place where the ancient Charing Cross stood. It may be of interest to note—where the modern one stands is on the ground where the regicides suffered execution on the Restoration of Charles II.

If this were the place for moralizing, we might consider how little this great soldier and politician, Edward, could have dreamed that a later age would destroy these beautiful memorials of a great love to Eleanor his queen! They could not be classed, by any age, as a superstition—unless a great human love is a superstition—if so, let us all pray to be superstitious! They were not like some others, as Preaching Crosses, where monks of the old faith inculcated their doctrines; nor were they Weeping Crosses, where in days long passed sinners knelt and with tears of contrition did bitter penance—they were solely memorial of a deep and passionate love that would—the lover-king thought—defy Time.

And here we are insensibly called to remember two other long processions of loved ones who were dead. In Spain, all through many nights, from Burgos, where he died, to Granada, where he was buried, Joanna la Loca, the mad Queen of Castile,

had carried her young husband, Philip of **Flanders**.
In England, in a later age, the decapitated Lord
Derwentwater was carried by his household at night,
with gleaming flambeaux, from London, where he
suffered, to his own Castle of Dilston, where he was
laid at rest. Yet in both these latter cases no
memorials were set up to mark where their beloved
ashes rested in their transit. Well, if for no other
reason than for art's sake, we must be thankful to
King Edward that three of these lovely crosses of his
love still remain with us!

Again, at an earlier period than that of Edward I,
if the Chronicle of William of Malmesbury is to be
believed, Aldhelm, the celebrated Saxon saint, died at
fifty miles distance from the Abbey of Glastonbury,
where he was to be buried; at each stage of seven
miles where the body rested, a cross was afterwards
erected. At these crosses, we are told by the same
chronicler, the sick were cured, and seven were
standing in his day and were called " Bishop stones."
(Gesta Pontif, p. 282.)

We have at the beginning of this paper mentioned
that the first Christian Emperor, Constantine, ordered
crosses to be erected, instead of the pagan emblems,
as terminals, to mark off different lands and ownerships.
These " Boundary Crosses" were in the same way
used in the early Middle Ages and Saxon times to
mark off the limits of the ground. There are
references in old charters to various " Boundary
Crosses," in which they are referred to as " a gilded
cross," " a wooden cross," " a stone cross," " a red

cross," and sometimes merely as a " Christ Symbol." These served to mark the limits of Church property. So the monks of Edmundsbury (Dugdale, " Monasticon," 3.99) erected four crosses, one at each extremity of the town, to define the limits of their authority, and Bishop Losinga raised a cross at Norwich to serve as a boundary mark between the land of the Church and the borough. St. Guthlac also set up a cross at Croyland for the same purpose as a boundary mark.

There is an Irish canon of the eighth century which directs that a Cross should be set up on all consecrated grounds, not only to mark the bounds but also to sanctify the spot.

A few centuries later in England, a law had to be passed forbidding men to set up a cross falsely upon their lands that was to pass them off as Church property, and so evade taxation. (Seymour, p. 321.)

To these Boundary Crosses of the Church land, " Rogation " processions were made, when the clergy went and laid earth and grass upon the boundary stones and offered prayers to avert pestilence.

Again, at these Boundary Crosses was generally the place chosen by his friends, particularly if he belonged to a Guild, for the medieval pilgrim to one of the shrines in this country or overseas to the Holy Land, to be wished " God-speed." So in the " Gild of the Resurrection " of Lincoln, it was ordained in 1374, " If any brother or sister wishes to make the pilgrimage to Rome, St. James of Galicia or the Holy Land, he shall forewarn the Gild and all the brethren

and sisters shall go with him and each shall give him
a half-penny at the least." The same rule is found in
the Gild of the Fullers at Lincoln founded in 1297—
the pilgrim going to Rome was accompanied as far as
the Queen's Cross outside the town if he left on a
Sunday or a feast day.

Kindred to these " Boundary Crosses " were those
set up with " sanctuary " privileges. Some Churches,
out of special reverence for the saints whose
relics they possessed, had this peculiar privilege of
" sanctuary," hence stone crosses were set up to show
to the man seeking sanctuary when he entered the
ground which was inviolable to the operation of the
civil law.

In Saxon times a chair of stone called " The Frid
or Frith stool " was sometimes also set up near the
shrines by the High Altar; the Churches of York,
Hexham, and Beverley enjoyed this privilege, and in
the last, two " stools " may still be seen. The rights
of the " Frith stool" overshadowed the whole region
for the distance of a mile, hence the stone crosses were
set up on the margin of this sanctuary region to mark
the limits of safety to the runaway miscreant. This
custom is noticed in the dying wish of St. Cuthbert,
who desired to be buried at Farne Island, lest if buried
at Lindisfarne, whence from the mainland there was a
causeway, his grave might become a place of refuge
for these runaways from justice. (Rock 3, part 1,
p. 365.)

These crosses stood very high, so that the fugitive
could see them from afar and be guided to safety.

A cross gave sanctuary sometimes even to animals. Thus Basolus, in the hill country of Rheims, becoming a hermit, a bear took refuge in his cell which was protected with sanctuary rights; the hunter left it in peace, and this seems a fact, not a legend, as four centuries after, by an agreement of hunters, the game hunted in the forest of Rheims was always spared when it touched on the little wood over which the Cross of St. Basle proclaimed sanctuary. (Montalembert, " Monks of the West," V, ii, p. 349.)

As to simple Wayside Crosses, Shakespeare reminds us of one of their uses when in the " Merchant of Venice " he makes Stephano apologize to Lorenzo for the absence of Portia:

> " She doth stray about
> By holy Crosses, where she kneels and prays
> For happy wedlock hours."

Again in the " Merry Devil of Edmonton " the father accounts for the delay in a wedding:

> " But there are Crosses, wife; here's one in Waltham,
> Another at the Abbey, and the third
> At Chester, and it's ominous to pass
> Any of these without a Paternoster."

So of Memorial Crosses, these words in " Marmion " will occur to us:

> " Half he murmured—
> ' Is there none
> Of all my halls have nursed,
> Page, squire or groom, one cup to bring'
> Of blessed water from the spring
> To slake my dying thirst? ' "

Clara, in the poem, forgets her wrongs.

" But where shall she turn ?   Behold her mark
  A little fountain cell,
Where waters clear as diamond-spark
  In a stone basin fell.
Above, some half-worn letters say, [on the pedestal of
    the cross]
' Drink, weary pilgrim, drink and pray
For the kind soul of Sybil Gray
  Who built this Cross and well.' "

A Wayside Cross was set up by the FitzWilliam family, which was standing about 1520, engraved on it :

" Whoso is hungry, and lists to all
  Let him come to Sprodburgh to his meate;
And for a night, and for a day
His horse shall have both corn and hay,
And no man shall ask him where he goes away."
          —Stamford's " Great Governing Families of
            England," Vol. I, p. 125.

Somewhat akin to " Weeping Crosses " are the so-called " Crosses of Absolution." These were not erected as others we have mentioned, outside or upright, but as our forefathers would extend the virtues and powers of the Cross, even beyond life, are found in sepulchres with an absolution engraved on them. Thus in the ancient Church of Butteils, near Dieppe, several skeletons exhumed were found bearing on their breasts rudely-cut crosses of sheet-lead, on which words of absolution occurred.

In our own country such have been found at Bury
St. Edmunds, Chichester and elsewhere. One of a
bishop dated 1088 is still at Chichester. In the annals
of the Benedictine Order of Cluny it is recorded when
Abelard died in 1142, Heloise applied to the Abbot
for such. It was granted (the absolution) as it
appears, as a matter of course, hence it may be inferred
these Absolution Crosses were not at all unusual.

Sometimes the Cross of Absolution was not placed
on the dead, and to induce prayers for his soul an
Indulgence was offered to any who thus charitably
should pray for him. Thus Dugdale, in his
" Baronage," records that in Lewes Priory a pardon-
epitaph was appended to John, seventh Earl
Warren's tomb; it was in verse and concluded with the
following couplet:

> " Ki pur sa alme priera
> Troiz mil jeurs de pardon avera."

So on the slab of a brass to Reynaud Alard, 1354,
at Winchelsea, the inscription winds up with an
Indulgence to him who prays for Reynaud Alard's
soul, " qe pur salme priera L jours de pardon avera."

Briefly has now been recounted the many different
crosses found in the Middle Ages in this land of ours,
namely—Wayside, Market, Preaching, Weeping,
Memorial and Sanctuary Crosses—also the useful
Boundary Crosses, and it may be asked what use,
except a purely archæological one, is the consideration
of them at the present day?

D

There is, since the Great War ended, more than an archæological reason for their consideration and study. Throughout these isles of ours—as also in France and Belgium, memorials of our fallen warriors are being continuously designed and set up. How useful for art's sake if the remains of the beautiful old Stone Crosses were copied—instead of the disfiguring and inartistic memorials now set up! If the piety which wielded the ancient chisel and dominated the ancient designer of these lovely Crosses is no more—if their present-day construction is by contract with a mason who knows nothing of art—at least, these remains of an age when individual pride in work and design was everywhere might well be copied with the very best results.

Take one instance. There was in the ancient town of Abingdon—till Cromwell's time—a most lovely Gothic Cross. We are told the lieutenant of the Roundhead soldiers—who were told to demolish it—shed tears over its destruction—not a vestige remains, but pictures of it are still extant. Instead of copying these—a year or two ago—a hideous plinth, like a box or marble dining-room clock, the townsfolk have erected to their fallen men.

In a neighbouring village, the lord of the manor has designed and set up on the village green a memorial like a cheese-churn.

Now these are only two examples of what is being done—and done to hand on to after ages—in these contract-made and devoid-of-art memorials to our Dead, when if well-directed copies of the four Eleanor

Crosses—or those in Iona—or even Ireland were made—a thing of beauty, so a joy for ever, would find place in our towns and villages. Poverty cannot be used as a justification of these stone-horrors. The Middle Ages, when the Crosses were works of beauty, were far poorer than our own. Yet in the then village of Liverpool alone, six stone crosses of remarkable beauty were erected, and so on in other towns and villages throughout Britain.

In connection with Memorial Crosses in Great Britain, some reference might be made to the last memorial of a battle; in such we refer to that placed over the fallen soldiers far north at Glansmuir (Culloden). The only memorial is a large and rude cairn over them of stones.

It was a very usual way in Norse countries of commemorating the dead, so remains of such tumuli are many. It is said the first stone beginning this cairn was made by a passing tinker! Whether that be so or not the writer does not know.

The cairn from accumulation of stones is now large—but who, if only for the sake of romance and no glorification of loyalty, would not desire to see a replica of the Cross of Iona, or even an Eleanor Cross, raised in memory of these brave lads, particularly as with a few exceptions they were of the Catholic faith, or perhaps here, if anywhere, a Weeping Cross, copied of old, might be placed—to catch the tears of a wandering pilgrim over a lost Cause that went down —as a setting sun—in the glory of a blood-red sky.

However, we must leave this interestng subject of

the old Stone Crosses of this land—some now intact, others found embedded in the earth, others used as stones in village walls and houses, and as we note their lingering beauty in decay few will not murmur the poet's words about those who erected them:

" Firm was their faith, the ancient band,
    The wise of heart in wood and stone,
Who reared with stern and trusting hands
    These Crosses in the days unknown.
They filled the land with many a thought,
    They bade each nook a truth recall,
The pillared stone its legend brought,
    A Doctrine came from roof and wall."

SANCTUARY KNOCKER, ALL SAINTS' CHURCH, HIGH OUSEGATE.

SANCTUARIES

In old England — covered with dense forests, impassable roads, outlaws lurking in the woods—often might be seen a man dishevelled, panting, almost spent, faltering yet urging his weary feet still on, because behind him came the avenger of his crimes.

To such the lights showing through the forest of distant Durham or Beverley were very angels of comfort and peace—once at their doors he was for a time safe.

Even convent churches which might not have the royal mandate to be sanctuaries for the flying felon, but were only consecrated and so possessed a certain harborage of safety, were often used if stately Durham or Beverley or Hexham, or in the south Beaulieu or St. Martin-le-Grand, were not nigh by the felon. Such Browning saw in his mind's eye when he wrote:

" The breathless fellow at the Altar foot
    Fresh from his murder, safe and sitting there
    With the little children round him in a row
    Of admiration, half for his beard and half
    For that white anger of his victim's son
    Shaking a fist at him with one fierce arm,
    Signing himself with the other because of Christ
    Whose sad Face on the Cross sees only this
    After the passion of a thousand years."

Sanctuary is said by ancient writers to have been first established in this island by Lucius, King of Britain, who is reported to have lived in the third century of the Christian era, but whose very existence is doubtful. Spelman states that Pope Boniface the Fifth was the first who commanded altars and palaces to be places of refuge for offenders. This was probably in imitation of the ordinance of Moses, which appointed three cities as a refuge for him " who should kill his neighbour unawares."

There were two kinds of sanctuary, one of a temporary and limited, another of a permanent and general nature. It must be borne in mind that almost any crime except malicious homicide could be compromised under the Saxon laws for a stated sum of money, so sanctuary appears at first to have been only intended to afford a temporary refuge for criminals till they could compromise their offence with their accusers.

In a Council held under Ina, King of the West Saxons (A.D. 698), it was decreed that if anyone guilty of a capital crime took refuge in a church, his life should be spared, but that he should make amends as the case demanded, if his offence was of a nature only punishable with stripes, the stripes should be forgiven him.

By the laws of King Alfred (A.D. 887) it was ordained that if a man were guilty of a small offence and fled to a church which did not belong to the king or the family of a private person, he should be allowed three nights to provide for himself elsewhere, unless he could in the meantime make his peace.

" That if during these three days anyone should assault or ill-treat him, that person should so violating the rights of sanctuary, pay the malefactor's life ransom and one hundred and twenty shillings to the Clergy of the sanctuary Church."

The Saxon laws went even further in pity to the flying felon—it was decreed that whoever should fly to a church and confess from a penitential reverence of God any crime of which he had been guilty, the penalty of such crime should be remitted him.

On the whole, therefore, it may be concluded that from the time of the Saxon kings, under modifications, churches and churchyards were a refuge for offenders, and the privileges of the temporal sanctuary were in them to be found.

Henry II, at the Council of Clarendon, extended the time of sanctuary to forty days and granted to those taking refuge there, during those forty days, that they should be defended by the Church officers and also by the townsfolk of any neighbouring town.

The chief sanctuaries in the realm were at Durham, Beverley, Hexham, Beaulieu, and St. Martin-le-Grand, London.

The manner of receiving fugitives differed somewhat at these several sanctuaries.

At Durham it was thus:

(1) The fugitive was at the north door. There were two chambers where men slept to receive fugitives at any hour of the night.

(2) He was admitted at that late hour of the night and the Galilee bell was tolled to give notice that someone had, as it was termed, taken Church, i.e. Sanctuary.

(3) The fugitive was required to declare why he had taken sanctuary and this before credible witnesses —also the nature of his offence.

(4) He had then to toll a bell in token of his demand for sanctuary.

(5) He then put on a gown of black cloth with a yellow X (cross) called St. Cuthbert's upon the left shoulder. A grate or bedstead was then provided him near the opposite (south) door of the Galilee, as it was called, and then for thirty-seven days he was provided at the expense of the house with sufficiency of provision and bedding.

At Beverley the proceedings were rather different. The felon taking sanctuary there (the rights of sanctuary there having been granted by Athelstan in A.D. 937) had to assent to the following:

(1) Ye shall be true and faithful to the Archbishop of York and to the Canons of the Church.

(2) Ye shall bear good heart to the Baillie and Governor of this town.

(3) Ye shall bear no pointed weapon, dagger or knife, against the king's peace.

(4) If any fire break out ye shall help to suppress it.

(5) Ye shall be ready at the Obit of King Athelstan at the Dirge and Mass and help to ring the bell for such.

He then had to kiss the book (of the Evangel),

to pay the bailiff's fee, and the clerk for his name to be put on the Register.

At Beverley also persons of distinction taking sanctuary had a lodging in the dormitory or a house in the precincts, and their privileges extended to the border of the county.

If anyone remained in sanctuary after forty days, he was debarred of the power of abjuration, after which time it was not lawful for anyone to give him food.

Complaints having been made to Edward II that those who sought refuge in sanctuaries were so closely watched by their enemies armed in the churchyards that they could not obtain food or even satisfy the wants of nature, nor depart from the hallowed ground when at the expiration of forty days they had to fulfil their oath of abjuration and seek ship out of the realm, it was commanded they should be allowed liberty for these purposes, and all men—their enemies included —should consider them, under dire penalties, to be in the king's peace and protection.

The abjuration all such felons took in whatever sanctuary they were for the forty days sheltered, was as follows:

" This hear, O Coroner, that I, M or N, am a stealer of sheep or of any other beast, or a murderer of one or more, and because I have done many such evils and robberies in the land I do abjure the land of our Lord the King of England, and I shall haste me towards the port of such place which thou hast given me, and that I shall not go out on the highway, and

if I do, I will that I be taken as a robber and a felon
of our Lord the King, and that at such a place I will
diligently seek for passage and that I will tarry there
but one flood and ebb, if I can have passage; and
unless I can have it in such a place I will go every day
into the sea up to my knees, assaying to pass over, and
unless I can do this within forty days I will put myself
again into the Church, as a robber and a felon of our
Lord the King, so God help me and his Holy
Judgment."

Much later it may be interesting to note that
Catholic recusants, according to Wilkinson in his
" Office of Coroners " (p. 41, 1641), made a similar
abjuration as follows:

" This hear you, Sir Coroner, that I, of M or H
in the county of S, am a Popish Recusant, and in
contempt of the laws and statutes of this Realm of
England, I have and do refuse to come to hear Divine
Service there read and exercised; I do therefore,
according to the intent and meaning of the Statute
made in the XXXV of Queen Elizabeth, late Queen
of this Realm of England, Abjure the Law and Realm
of King James, now King of England, Scotland,
France and Ireland. And I shall haste me towards
the Port of P which you have given and assigned to
me, and that I shall not go out of the highway leading
thither nor return back again: and that if I do, I will
be taken as a felon of our said Lord the King, and that
at P I will diligently seek for passage and I will tarry
there but one flood and ebb, if I can have passage, and
unless I can have it in such space, I will go every day

into the sea up to my knees, assaying to pass over, so God help me and His Holy Judgment," etc.

Abjuration, though a crime against the Crown, was sometimes pardoned, thus in the patents of the fifteenth year of King John, that king pardons Roger de Parles for having abjured his realm.

It was necessary that the flying felon took good care that the refuge was in a true Church—duly consecrated, or he could claim no sanctuary rights; thus we find the question arise in a case of the time of Edward I reported in the Year Books of that reign (we give the translation):

" A certain man taken into custody for theft was brought before the Justices of the Peace, and he replied that he had taken refuge in a certain church whence he was seized and removed, and he claimed to be restored to such a church (of refuge); the Judge replied that to his knowledge the said church had never been consecrated by a bishop (and therefore had no sanctuary rights)."

If it had been it would have been sacrilege to have removed him, for such a church in the Middle Ages was a most sacred place: whoever had crossed its threshold was under the protection of God, and many fine miracles, which were then familiar among the people, attested with what particular favour the right of sanctuary was regarded by the Holy Virgin. At Walsingham, whither was a celebrated pilgrimage, people never failed to go and see the " Gate of the Knight," a gate which had stretched itself so as to give miraculous shelter to a man on horseback hard pressed by his enemies, and who found himself thus opportunely placed beyond the touch of men as well as beyond the reach of law.

A priest who took refuge in a church was—unlike a layman—not obliged to quit the realm; he swore that he was a priest and enjoyed ecclesiastical privilege according to the praiseworthy custom of the kingdom. (Statute of Ed. II, cap. 15.)

Till Henry VII obtained a Bull from the Pope, traitors could not be taken out of sanctuary; but the Church, as sacrilege in her eyes was the greatest of faults, permitted and gave up those in sanctuary who had been guilty of that crime. Thus in 1320 a woman who was named Isabel of Bury killed the priest of All Saints near London Wall and she remained in the church five days, thereupon the Bishop of London issued his letter in which he declared the rights of sanctuary would not save her; she was brought, therefore, out of the church to Newgate and hanged on the third day after. (Croniques de London.)

Sometimes a fugitive in sanctuary seems to have been taken out and then replaced, thus *temp.* Henry VIII: "At Richmond, in 1557, a letter arrived to the Abbot of Westminster to give orders that a certain Edmond Vaughan, at that time in sanctuary, who stood accused of various misdemeanours, be delivered to the Constable of the Tower and by him further to be examined, and afterwards signifying to the Abbot the said Vaughan shall be restored again to sanctuary."

.   .   .   .   .   .

Though we have seen by an instance given above that for the sin of sacrilege the Church refused to shield a felon who had committed that crime, yet if the felon was a traitor to the sovereign, she would not give him up to the civil courts or king; and as we have said, it was not till the reign of Henry VII, who was frequently assailed by traitors to his crown, that he procured by a Bull from Rome leave to apprehend any traitor who had taken refuge in a church. Yet we find in the turbulent reigns of our Plantagenet kings, these rights of sanctuary had often been invaded.

The most notorious case was that when the four knights burst into Canterbury Cathedral and slew Thomas à Becket, sprinkling his brains on the steps of the sanctuary.

In 1454 the Duke of Exeter, nearly akin to the king by descent from the Black Prince, took sanctuary at Westminster. To the horror of the Abbot, he was taken out by force.

Edward IV, after the Battle of Tewkesbury, when twenty persons of the Lancastrian army, including the Duke of Somerset and, according to some historians, Edward, Prince of Wales, had taken sanctuary in that Abbey, violated its rights and had them brought out and executed.

In 1232 Hubert de Burgh took sanctuary at Merton Abbey, afterwards at the small church of Brentwood in Essex, when he took the Cross in one hand and the Host in the other. The king's officers broke in upon him, seized him, chained his feet under his horse's belly and conducted him to the Tower.

We find the Dean and Chapter of St. Mary's, Stafford, petitioning the king in 1300 against certain persons who had seized men out of sanctuary in that church.

Sometimes, Drysdale tells us, churches were set on fire to compel sanctuary men to come forth. Of this the most striking case is that of William Fitz-Osbert, called William Longbeard, who was by these means forced to leave the Church of St. Mary-le-Bow. He was seized, mutilated and hanged.

These are a few instances where rights of sanctuary were often set aside in the Middle Ages, and in ages, too, when the Church and her holy places were looked on with fear and reverence.

An instance here may be given of a case where the Church refused to give up a traitor who had taken part in a well-known episode of history—in the Rebellion of Jack Cade, 1450, when one of his accomplices flew to St. Martin-le-Grand, the most famous of the southern sanctuaries. The king in this case wrote to the Dean of St. Martin's, ordering him to produce the traitor. This the Dean refused to do, and he exhibited his Charters, which, being found correct, the fugitive was allowed to remain in safety where he was. (From "Historical Notices of the Collegiate Church," by J. Kempe, 1825.)

According to Fleta (lib. I, cap. XXIX), at the end of forty days of asylum, if the malefactors had not taken the oath of abjuration, food must be denied them and they would no longer be allowed to emigrate. On the road to the port, according to the same authority, the felon wore a costume which would cause him to be recognized. He was to be " ungirt, unshod, bareheaded, in his bare shirt as if he were to be hanged on the gallows, having received a cross in his hands "—yet if he had taken the oath of abjuration, which entailed him seeking the seaport and exiling himself from the realm, no one on his way thither molested him—perhaps some out of pity, some in sympathy with his crimes, all in awe of the king's peace which he possessed.

Jusserand, the historian, gives an excerpt from the Durham Registers still in existence, which shows how in that one sanctuary alone, in sixty years, i.e., from 1464-1524, besides other crimes, two hundred and eighty-three persons had obtained sanctuary who were guilty of murders and homicides. They were chiefly common folk, but in the list were three ecclesiastics and one knight who had been accessory to the crime.

As Durham, Beverley and Hexham were the great sanctuaries of the North, so the greatest in the south, particularly as it was in the Metropolitan City, was the now destroyed Abbey or Collegiate Church of St. Martin-le-Grand. In a dense (for England at that time) population, with countless brawls going on in its crowded lanes and alleys, the immunities it offered as a sanctuary were constantly being seized on. The Abbey and schools founded in the reign of Edward the Confessor by two noble brothers—Ingelric and Girard—for secular canons, not only by Norman

William, but by his successors, received repeated benefactions and charters granting ample sanctuary rights.

But though often used by the innocently accused, as time went on and the simplicity of early days passed away and a lax of faith upgrew, hordes of profligate offenders took refuge within its privileged limits. Stowe writes of such in his Chronicle: " Now unthriftes riot and run in debt upon the boldness of these places, yea and rich men run thither with poor men's goods, there they bid their creditors go whistle for them. Men's wives run thither with their husband's plate and say they dare not abide their husband's for beating. Thieves bring thither their stolen goods. They devise new robberies and reeve and kill and come in again."

Henry VIII, to try and mitigate these excesses, ruled that sanctuary men were to wear badges and were not to go abroad before sun-rising or after sun-setting. By another Statute passed in the thirty-third year of this king, all privileged places, including St. Martin's, are extinguished except churches and churchyards, and as anciently, so now, anyone taking sanctuary was allowed forty days therein, but he is to be brought before the Coroner and branded, and not, as of old, to abjure the realm but to choose one particular sanctuary where he is to remain for life. This concession freeing him from being sent abroad was ordained in consequence of foreign realms having, through its operations, obtained in " these outlaws many expert mariners and soldiers, and many English in the use and practices of archers." (22 Henry VIII, cap. 141.)

Even this mitigated recognition of sanctuaries was done away with (theoretically at least) in the twenty-first year of King James I. "And be it also enacted by the authority of this present Parliament that no sanctuary, or privilege of sanctuary, shall be hereafter admitted or allowed in any case." This Act did not, however, totally suppress such, for in 1697 it was again enacted, and there were sanctuaries of sorts as late as the reign of George I, when the asylum of St. Peter's at Westminster was demolished.

The Abbey or Collegiate Church falling under the Act (Ed. VI), which surrendered all ecclesiastical conventual buildings into the power of the Crown, St. Martin's gradually became ruinous, so that after some centuries the ground was used to build the General Post Office in the city. In addition to St. Martin-le-Grand, several city churches in the Middle Ages also had refuges for malefactors—thus the Churches of St. Bride and St. Sepulchre. We find in 1324 ten felons escaped from Newgate; five were retaken, four escaped to St. Sepulchre's, one to St. Bride's—all these men took the oath of abjuration and fled abroad.

In ending this paragraph of city sanctuaries, because in novels and other works it has so often been mentioned as the ground of episodes in such fiction, the name of "Alsatia" must not be forgotten. Alsatia was the fancy name for the Sanctuary of White Friars or Carmelites in Fleet Street, which after the dis-

E

solution of monasteries came to be peopled with roaring blades, swaggering desperadoes, thieves of every grade, dissolute women and their bullies, gamesters and crowds of ruffians. The windows and buildings ruinous and falling into decay, instead of the ancient sanctuaries in churches where the flying miscreant heard the chants of the monks and holy voices in prayer, here in these secularized precincts, oaths and blasphemies on every side. White Friars Priory, afterwards the desecrated place called "Alsatia," had been founded in 1241 by Sir Richard Grey. In 16c8 the inhabitants of its ruined Priory obtained certain rights from James I of exemptions and privileges, which in time were taken advantage of by these dissolute people who pitched their dwelling there.

In enumerating the sanctuaries of the south, Westminster Abbey must not be omitted, this church having great privileges of sanctuary. In a note to this essay we give the Charter of such given by Edward the Confessor. From the Sanctuary and Abbey being near the Royal Palace—a king's palace having a sacredness which in this age we can hardly realize—it derived even greater respect than possibly others without such position. We all know the story of Richard, the uncle of the little son of Edward IV, going to this sanctuary where Queen Elizabeth had taken refuge, and how so sacred was held the rights of the Westminster Sanctuary, the prince dare not by force remove his nephew and only could effect it by persuasion. Its first privileges of sanctuary even

dated back further than the Confessor's time—to
Sebert, King of the East Saxons.

Several curious relics of English sanctuaries are
still in existence. There is at Durham the celebrated
bronze knocker still affixed to the Cathedral door,
chiselled in Norman times; holding this, even before
the door was opened, the flying felon was in safety.

At Beverley there was once a " fridstool " or peace
chair; this has gone, but the inscription is preserved.
" This stone seat is called ' freedstool,' that is, chair of
peace, on reaching which a fugitive criminal enjoys
complete safety." This privilege, as we shall see, at
Hexham extended not only to the church but to one
mile round it, the space being divided into six circles,
and it was more and more sinful to drag fugitives
violently from the sanctuary, the nearer they were
when seized to the inner circle.

In the choir of Hexham Abbey is a relic of really
exceptional interest, namely the original fridstole or
sanctuary chair, which is believed to have stood in
Wilfrid's Saxon Church—for the pious founder had
secured this right of refuge for his creation, the
boundaries extending about a mile all round it. The
limits were marked by four columns; the Hexham one
at first stood in the middle of the Tyne, but the floods
proving too much for it, precision had to be sacrificed,
and it was placed (so the chronicler Richard of
Hexham tells us) on the north bank. White-cross
fields on the east, and Maiden Cross on the west, still
recall the localities where two of the others stood.
The sanctity of these boundaries held good till the

time of Henry VII, and with modifications till that of James I. The old stone relic is thought to have served also as a consecration chair for the Hexham bishops, while Camden went further and held that the kings of Northumbria were crowned in it.

In summing up this review of sanctuaries we must remember, if in some particular cases they erred on the side of mercy, they were so far authorized encroachments upon the Royal prerogative of pardon which had always existed.

Again, we should not forget that the criminal who took sanctuary did not escape punishment; he had to abjure the realm, forfeit his goods and submit to a weary life-long banishment, far from his kith and kin, and by a late Statute of Henry VIII he was to carry his shame with him wherever he wandered, for he was ordered before he left the realm to be branded on the thumb.

Again, to a man taking sanctuary was afforded a respite in those rude ages of, often, summary justice, while his case could be debated by a dispassionate judge, instead of an excited and ignorant mob of avengers, hot on his heels, who had no time to judge his case fairly. How many innocent lives this breathing place in sanctuary saved! How many guilty souls that would have been summarily sent to their last account, it preserved to do better, if they would, in exile.

Speaking of this exile overseas the thought arises, where did these flying culprits go? Probably, as the nearest land and the easiest to find passage to, to France, or to the Angevin possession of our early kings. There some, religiously swayed, went on pilgrimage to Rome; others joined—if able-bodied— the troops of some restless Baron; others joined those Free Companies which, after the One Hundred Years' War, roamed over Europe.

Days have changed since then. If we now, because we do not want them, allowed our murderers, thieves and felons to escape abroad, they would soon be sent back by the political " parcel post " of those lands oversea—but no such samples or complications of international law then impeded their journeys. The immense parties, especially from these shores (for even in those days the English were addicted to wandering the earth), who on pilgrimage left these shores for other countries, facilitated the escape abroad of our undesirable population, and it was easy for them as soon as they embarked to throw over the distinctive garments of men escaped from sanctuary.

However, these men availing themselves of sanctuary—and that was one reason the Medieval Church in her mercy took them in—became sometimes reformed characters. Their hard hearts and savage natures were transformed into God-fearing and even saintly recluses, and the penitent thief became a saint.

Cæsarius of Hesterbach (*circa* 1220) in his " Dialogues " tells the story of one such converted when in peril of life. " In the days when King Otto went to Rome to be crowned Emperor, he committed the government of the Moselle lands to his brother Henry, Count Palatine, who solemnly sentenced to death a certain robber noble. But the Abbot of Schoenau arrived on the spot and besought the Count Palatine until he granted the robber his life. This man having escaped death by the grace of conversion, henceforth lived a good life, and he adds, many others became such too. And that after all should, then as now, whether in the sanctuaries of Holy Church in the past, or in our prisons of to-day, be the aim—not punishment, but reformation. And who knows that some day all those who have sorrowed and wept here, who have suffered hunger and thirst, fallen and risen again, though the old sanctuaries here below are now shattered and lost, who knows but they shall be gathered in to God's own Sanctuary, a Sanctuary not made with hands, eternal in the heavens?

NOTE

EDWARD THE CONFESSOR'S GRANT OF SANCTUARY TO WESTMINSTER

EDWARD, by the grace of God king of Englishmen: I make it to be known to all generations of the world after me, that by special commandment of our holy father Pope Leo, I have renewed and honoured the Holy Church of the blessed apostle St. Peter, of Westminster; and I order and establish for ever, that what person, of what condition or estate soever he be, from whence soever he come, or for what offence or cause it be, either for his refuge into the said holy place, he be assured of his life, liberty and limbs. And over this I forbid, under the paine of everlasting damnation, that no minister of mine, or of my successors, intermeddle them with any the goodes, lands or possessions of the said persons taking the said sanctuary—for I have taken their goodes and livelode into my special protection, and therefore I grant to every each of them, in as much as my terrestriall power may suffice, all manner freedom of joyous libertie; and whosoever presumes or doth contrary to this my grant, I will hee lose his name, worship, dignity and power, and that with the great traytor Judas that betraied our Saviour he be in the everlasting fire of hell; and I will and ordayne that this my grant endure as long as there remayneth in England eyther love or dread of Christian name."

TALISMANS

AT the time that talismans and amulets were in use, we need hardly remind the reader that there existed a general belief in omens and astrologers, fortune-tellers and prophets and soothsayers who, like those of old, advised upon the flight of birds or the appearance of the heavens, or on the inspection and use of rare plants and precious stones: all such practices were approaching wizardry, but not black magic, though our King James I had a saying which has passed into proverb, " Who sup with the devil hath need of long spoons." The almanack makers also of the Stuart period, such as Lily, Heydon, Partridge, and others, practised their calling, which included that of crystal-seeing and advice from the conjunction of planets. Oliver Cromwell is known to have believed in auspicious days, Archbishop Laud believed in omens and registered his dreams (Burnet, p. 17), and Charles I consulted astrologers at the principal periods of his life, and there is the well-known story of him using the old practice of sortilege with the leaves of the Bible, in the University library at Oxford. All the kings of this dynasty touched for the King's Evil, and there was then an old superstition, still found in the remoter parts of the Highlands, that the seventh

72

son of a seventh son had the miraculous touch also for healing and warding off fevers.

Chemists, not only in the early Middle Ages, but much later, believed in and sought for the philosopher's stone, whose touch would turn baser metal into gold. They believed in the curing of diseases by sympathetic powders, while of course the divining hazel rod to find water was then practised as it still is. The power of second sight and the evil eye were as commonly believed then as they are now in most parts of Italy and the East, therefore to counteract these and such-like uncanny things, it is easy to perceive how general were talismans and amulets.

Even as late as Monmouth's time it was reported as an ordinary circumstance, that when he was captured after Sedgemoor, many charms and spells were found tied about his person, while his tablet book was full of astrological figures that no one could understand. The Duke told Colonel Legge, who had been in custody, that he had got these various things from Scotland. (Burnet, p. 414.)

It was commonly believed in the sixteenth and seventeenth centuries that that pious maid, Joan of Arc, was a witch, and this seems to be the only palliation of the mode in which Shakespeare dealt with her character in the play of Henry VI.

It was also believed that Charlemagne's mistress enchanted him with a ring, which as long as she had about her, he could not suffer her dead body to be carried out of his chamber to be buried. A bishop (so the legend went) took this ring out of her mouth and

threw it into a pond. Alas for the Emperor, his
chiefest pleasure after that was ever walking round
and round the lake which held the enchanted ring.

A legend of a somewhat similar type is recorded of
Sir Robert Tresilian, Chief Justice of England,
executed for treason in 1388, of whom, in the State
Trials, it is reported that when he came to the place of
execution he said, " As long as I doe wear anything
upon me, I shall not die," whereupon the executioner
stripped him and found " certain images painted like
to the signs of the heavens, and the head of a devil
painted and the names of many of the devils wrote in
parchment." These being taken away, he was strung
up naked at Tyburn, where he was hanged. (State
Trials, Vol. I, p. 117.)

Before we inquire more intimately into the use of
such things as talismans and amulets, it may be of
interest to note that such still are in vogue, and from
time to time appear above the surface of these matter-
of-fact days.

An intelligent writer during the last great war
mentions how in a part of South London he met a
wounded soldier who denied all knowledge of charms,
yet after being questioned more closely admitted he
had seen farthings sewn into a soldier's collar or braces,
and that he himself wore one always sewn into his belt.
The same writer affirms a hospital nurse at Eastbourne
told him how her parents and brother and a friend,
just before they were returning to the front in Flanders,
were playing at cards, and one of these slipped out
of the pack. " That's luck," one of the party called

out, and tearing the card up into four pieces as a charm, handed each fourth piece to the rest.   They all kept a piece except the friend, who scornfully rejected it, throwing it into the fire.   The others all returned safely from the war, the one who rejected the charmed card was made a prisoner at the front.

Another story somewhat similar is this: During the war two wounded men were returned and seated on a bench at Eastbourne.   Being questioned, one of them showed an old farthing he had carried all through action as a charm, the other produced a small bag in which was a glass eye of a large animal; he said it was his charm against mishap in the war, and strongly believed in its efficacy.

From these anecdotes it can be seen that the ancient belief in charms or talismans has not yet died out, for it is the offshoot of long ago, when this efficacy and use obtained, and particularly so with soldiers as most exposed to unforeseen dangers.

As early as the days of Philip the Fair of France, ordinances of his were promulgated forbidding their use.   " A soldier," one such runs, " is to have no such pieces of stone or magical herbs or invocations on him, he is to rely only on God, his Right, his body, his horse and his arms."   But more gruesome charms were sometimes employed.   Thus an ancient annalist[1] informs us certain soldiers clothed themselves against evils in battle with a horrible vest called " a shirt of hell," figured over with demons and invocations.   To counteract such use of evil charms, a very frequent

[1] " Disquisitio Verum Magicarum," Ed. Lugdani, 1608.

good one was employed: it consisted in a script with written holy words on it. The old traveller Mandeville says not alone against evils in war, but against thieves it was employed; says he—" and therefore seyen some men when thei dreden them of thefes on any way or enemies." The words inscribed on these scripts were taken from the Gospel—" Jesus transient per medium illorum ibat " (Jesus passed through the midst of them), and so old Mandeville comments on them by saying, " Our Lorde passed through out of the Jewes countrie and escaped safely fro men."

A curious circumstance arises about these charmed words. They are found on the first Rose noble coin struck by our King Edward III. Now were these words magical or simply commemorating Edward III's escape at the sea-fight off Sluys? Were they, on the other hand, a talisman prescribed by Edward's favourite alchemist, Raymond Lulle? It seems to the writer that the latter is the most probable explanation, for these words were well known and used as magical words at that time, and if the king had merely wished to record his victory over his enemy at the sea-fight of Sluys, why did he choose those very words employed by many as magical, rather than some religious emblem, such as the alpha and omega which appears on the coins of Ethelred II or crosses as on the Byzantine coins? That Edward III used and believed in these magical things we have further proof of in an amulet of his with words formed of that character, which words occur in the book called the " Enchiridion," falsely attributed to Pope Leo III, which besides containing many prayers of St. Augustine, of St. Cyprian and others, contains also many blessings, charms and incantations to preserve against all sorts of dangers in war and turn the weapon of an enemy. One such we give: " Conjuro vos omnia genera armorum, gladios, cultellos, sagittas, glandes, catapultas, bipennes, lanceas, clavos et omnia armorum et metallorum, per Patrem et Filium et Spiritum Sanctum, ut non laedates me!"

Words written on scripts were the most in favour with soldiers, or else herbs or small stones which they could conceal under their armour. We have an instance of this in the case of one of two champions in a judicial duel in the reign of Edward III, the principals in which were the Bishop of Salisbury and the Earl of Salisbury, but forasmuch as the Bishop being an ecclesiastic could not himself fight, his appointed champion appeared in his stead, while the Earl appointed also his to meet him. When according to such contests the officials before it began examined each champion to see they only had legitimate arms about them, they found the Bishop's man had several scripts concealed about him inscribed with prayers and magical spells sewn in his clothes, and these being liable to give him an unfair advantage against the opposite champion, the Bishop was disqualified and the Earl won his case. (Year Book of Ed. III, Rolls Series, anno XXIX.)

A talisman that had a very extensive reputation in these Middle Ages was the strange mystical cross called the " Swastika." It seems to have obtained in

many countries and at many times.   It is found even
in the old ruins of India and China, and found too on
coins and inscriptions long before the Christian era.
To soldiers applying for magical preservatives it was
considered most efficacious, its belief as such founded
on long ages, hence its frequency on all sorts of
talismans.   Again, to protect in battle, possibly for
those who feared to employ magic, a more religious
charm was found.   John German, Bishop of Nocera,
in 1460 mentions that some soldiers fasted from the
Wednesday to the following day, declaring that if they
did this they would never be wounded in battle :
" Affermans que en ce abstenans ilz ne seront jamais
bleciez en bataille."   And then again, instead of
using the magical swastika or inscribed charms, hung
about their necks medals of the Agnus Dei.

Others entering battle reverted to more doubtful
charms.   In the probably fictitious " Gremoire " of
natural magic, ascribed to Pope Honorius III, are
several " formularies " for using charms or magical
words on swords against mishaps to the users.   Such
have been found on two swords, one at Lincoln, the
other, in France, at St. Omer.   The words placed
on these swords, and, of course, on many now
undiscovered, were " cabalistic," i.e., the words " Ibel,
Ebel, Abel," so used.   The parchment these magical
words had to be inscribed on, according to this
Gremoire of Honorius, was to be of a peculiar sort—
it must be provided from a clean animal and a young
one, unable from its youth to be bred from, a young
lamb or a kid or some creature of that sort.

Again, a very famous magical charm written on
script to ward off evil of every disease and wounds in
battle was the famous abracadabra—a cone of letters
consisting of A B C D, which could be read either
way the same. The first mention of it seems to be on
a medical poem written by Serenus Sammonicus, who
lived in the third century in the reign of the Emperor
Gordian the Younger. Defoe, writing as late as the
eighteenth century (1722), alludes to this strange
talisman as still in use (Defoe's "Journal of the
Plague Year ").

Another curious charm which was extensively
used in medieval times as an amulet consisted of five
Latin words so arranged that they could be read
backwards or forwards and also upwards and
downwards. These words were:

```
S A T O R
A R E P O
T E N E T
O P E R A
R O T A S
```

This charm has been found above the chapel of
St. Laurent at Rochemaur, France, and also in the
plaster wall of an old Roman house at Cirencester,
Gloucestershire. In the Bibliothèque Nationale,
Paris, is a translation, i.e.,

> The Sower
> The Plough
> Words
> Works
> Wheels

This charm appears in a manuscript of the fourteenth century of Italian origin, where it is recommended to be used for a speedy delivery.

As has been mentioned before, the use of script with these magical letters or incantations on them, owing to the ease they could be stowed away under the soldier's harness or the civilian's cloak from prying eyes, were greatly in favour in the Middle Ages, but there were others as convenient in size and more ostentatious in the wearing. We refer to jewels or precious stones. These were eminently ornamental to the possessor and very different to the dried frog an old woman on the Berkshire Downs some years ago recommended to the writer to wear on a string round his neck as a charm against tooth-ache!

Before mentioning some of the chief precious stones that our forefathers valued for their talismanic properties, it may not be uninteresting to inquire the reasons possibly stones of this kind were supposed to be so endowed.

(1) If it were not that in ancient Mexico, Assyria and the most ancient of Eastern Empires—now a mass of ruins—stones with magical words or numbers have been discovered, it would have been a fair deduction that through the Jews, who were the great traffickers for such precious gems in the Middle Ages, the mystical stones set in the " breastplate of judgment " in their ancient High Priest's bosom would have been the origin of this belief in the mystic power of rare jewels, but as we have said above, as races even older

than the Jewish treasured stones as magical, this derivation does not seem to hold.

(2) In the Middle Ages the dream of all alchemists and chemists was the discovery, if possible, of the " Philosopher's Stone," which, if once found, should render the forming of gold from the lower metals an accomplished fact. Now all these researches of the alchemists were made, as they began, and finished their investigations, with, and under magical words and spells. It is not therefore a long step from them—that constantly engaged with mineral bodies and strange chemicals, the alchemists should transfer to certain substances, and those the rarest, certain occult properties, particularly as their incessant search for a stone—the Philosopher's—was to possess those mysterious properties.

(3) The third hypothesis is that this belief in stones possessing magical powers has been handed down from the remotest era of the human race, when our savage progenitors, finding stones of curious shape and colour (as several savage races still do) treated them as of divine substance and treasured them on having magic powers.

If any of this be true, we need hardly fall back on a learned mineralogist (U. F. Brückman, 1737) who believed in the inherent chemical power of precious stones of sorts. "If," he writes, "any stone of this kind has more effect than an ordinary earthy substance, it is the lapis-lazuli, though," he adds, "we have a hundred other remedies cheaper." He testifies he has often seen these cheaper stones tendered by

F

apothecaries, thus " a yellow feldspar offered instead of a jacinth, and poor garnets as substitutes for rubies ! " Another eighteenth century philosopher propounds whether certain stones have, if worn, the power of throwing off upon the wearer of them some chemical properties—this seems a sort of foresight of radium!

Some of these talisman-jewels were the following :

(1) The diamond was considered a talisman in battle : as such it was worn (on the occasion evidently a failure) on the finger of King John of France taken prisoner by the Black Prince and by him transferred to the English Crown. A writer in the eleventh century states also from its clear and white colour it had the power of quenching the heat of certain fevers.

(2) Another powerful talisman was supposed to be the ruby. One of the finest is now in the crown of our present king. Originally it belonged to Abue Said, King of Granada. Unfortunately for him it was coveted by Pedro the Cruel, who murdered the Moorish king to obtain it. It afterwards was given by Henrique, Pedro's bastard brother, to Edward the Black Prince for his help to seat him on his brother's throne. The ruby stone was also considered a talisman of good fortune, though it had the power of changing its colour at the approach of ill to the wearer. Thus it is said that the one in the ring of unfortunate Catherine of Aragon changed colour when the question of her divorce was mooted.

(3) The sapphire—this beautiful stone was looked

upon as possessing always great talismanic and strange powers. It was accounted to possess a charm against unchastity. Therefore Pope Innocent III commanded for this reason all Bishops to wear a sapphire ring. It was further regarded as a scare against devils and the powers of evil. Even the Great Doctor of the Church—St. Jerome—wrote that the sapphire saved anyone, if such wore it, from captivity and made peace with foes.

(4) The amethyst was also used as a powerful talisman. In the opinion of a German writer of the eleventh or twelfth century, if worn by a man it attracted to him the love of noble women and also protected him from the attacks of thieves (Birlinger in " Germania," Vol. III). As a testimony of the belief in its efficacy prevalent at the opening of the fifteenth century may be noted its presence in the manuscript book of Marguerite of Flanders, Duchess of Burgundy, entitled " the book of the properties of certain stories." (Inventaire des Biens de Marguerite de Flandres.)

(5) The jacinth—this was much prized for its magical worth; among its many virtues it was said to protect from poison and melancholia and to make the wearer beloved of God and man. The following lines may serve to show how highly jasper was esteemed in old days as a talisman:

> " Auro quid melius? Jaspis.
> Quid jaspis? Virtus.
> Quid virtute? Deus.
> Quid Deitate? Nihil."

(What is better than gold? Jasper.
What is better than jasper? Virtue.
What is better than virtue? God.
What is better than the Deity? Nothing.)
—" Curieuse Kunst und Werek-Schul,"
Nuremberg, 1705, p. 994.

(6) The turquoise again was a good talisman
because it was believed to be very useful to the
wearer as changing its colour according to the owner's
health. In this way it was a sort of pocket doctor.
In these days, too, it might be very useful if, as it
was supposed to be able to do, it detected the fidelity
of a wife! Poets have sung its praises. Shakespeare
makes Shylock say he would not have lost his
turquoise for " a wilderness of monkeys," and the poet
Donne mentions its sympathetic qualities—" as a
compassionate turquoise that doth tell, by looking
pale, the wearer is not well."

If a man fell off his horse, too, having a ring of
turquoise, though the stone became broken, the man
received no hurt.

That Queen Elizabeth clung fondly to life is well
known, and it is said that she trusted much in the
virtues of a talisman she ever wore round her neck.
This was a piece of gold engraved with certain magic
characters.

The statement has also been made that at the
bottom of a chair in which she often sat, was the queen
of hearts from a pack of cards, having a nail driven
through the forehead of the figure. Evidently a spell
of some sort of witchcraft. Could it have been made

against her rival, Mary of Scotland? (See Agnes Strickland's " Lives of the Queens of England.")

(7) The white chalcedony was another talisman; even as long back as the Iron Age, such remnants of it have been found. If not the real jewel, then white stones to take its place have frequently been also found in tumuli in this and other northern nations. In Italy the superstition is that milky white chalcedony worn by the peasant farmers' wives increases the supply of the cows' milk, hence the Italian name for such a bead—" pietra lattea." This stone was much worn by the ancient Greeks and Romans as a talisman. There is a passage in the New Testament in the Book of the Apocalypse which seems to hint at such—" to him who overcometh will I give a white stone and on the stone a new name written which no man knoweth save to him that receiveth it." In the original Greek the word stone is " gem," which certainly seems to hint at the gem-like white chalcedony.

Another talismanic stone was the hyacinth: this, as a charm, preserved a person wearing it from thunder and lightning. It was a veritable miraculous stone according to M. Jacob (Sciences Occultes, Paris, 1862): it preserved persons from the plague, it rocked people to sleep. It was a stone that differed somewhat in colour; its most efficacious colour was red. It was so powerful in its magic that " il sembre estre quelque chose."

It would take up too much space to go further through the many precious stones which in the Middle Ages and much further back in the world's history were prized and looked on as talismans possessing magical properties. Of all such charms perhaps they were most pleasant to the wearers as not only ornaments but encouragers when worn of a feeling of magical protection. Far more pleasant, for instance, than a piece of the human skull which, removed when a person was trepanned, was frequently taken from it and used as a powerful talisman.

In this review of talismans and amulets the reader, as they are so associated always with magic, may wonder no reference is made to " Spells." The reason of this is that spells, which are spoken incantations, do not come under talismans or amulets: the latter were always tangible objects.

We will give three instances of spells, in which it will be seen in two of them no magical article passed into the keeping of the person seeking the curative charm, whereas if it had been a talisman, such would have carried away a script with words of power on it to wear in person, or a magical jewel or herb.

(1) The first " spell " is for " staunching blood." The one performing the charm shall say to the patient: " Our Saviour was born in Bethlehem Judah. As He passed by the river of Jordan the water would wave all in one, the Lord rise up His holy hand and bid the waters still to stand, and so shall thy blood. Amen."

(2) For a thorn in the finger: " Our Saviour was fastened to the Cross with nails and thorns which neither rots nor rankles. No more shan't thy finger." (This to be repeated three times.)

(3) To cure a wart: " Take a not (knot) of a reed

and strike the warts downwards three times and bury the reed." (In this spell it will be seen an object is used, so the reed becomes a talisman.)

Besides other talismans in jewels and scripts with magical words written on them, we find in these ages certain herbs were also used as such. In this article we referred to the case of the Bishop's champion, who, with other charms, had such concealed on his person and so was disqualified. Among these plants or herbs considered to be possessed of magical power and therefore often dried and either used singly or mixed together and carried about the person, were marigold flowers, sprigs of marjoram or thyme and wormwood. The vervain plant was also dried and used as a counter-charm against disease, and also spells cast by practisers of the Black Art. It had a long ancestry in such potentialities for it was sacred among the Greeks and Druids.

Rue was also looked on as having magical and medicinal powers. Powdered, it formed talismans, probably kept in little bags. It was supposed to bestow second sight, also to clear dim eyes; so sacred was the regard in which it once was held in these islands that we find the early Christian missionaries sprinkling holy water from brushes made of it, for which cause it got called "Herb of Grace." The poet Drayton refers to it in an incantation:

> " Then sprinkled she the juice of rue
> With nine drops of the midnight dew."

Then there was the fern; this was, if ground up

into a powder as the rue, a very powerful charm and talisman. Our ancestors could not understand this plant, which seemed to them to have neither flower nor seed, so they boldly asserted it had neither, and its growth therefore was a mystery, and as they saw it with no organs of fructification visibly increase, they judged it had the power in itself of invisibility and could confer such on the bearers of it. So in an old calendar of the Catholic Church, under date June 23rd and 24th, we read:

"Fern in great estimation with the vulgar, on account of its seed. Herbs of different kinds are sought with many ceremonies. Girl's thistle is gathered and a hundred crosses by the same. The nativity of John the Baptist. Dew and new leaves are in estimation."

In Ben Jonson's play "New Inn" we find an instance of the fern kept in a man's pocket as a talisman:

> " . . . I had
> No medicine, Sir, to go invisible,
> No fern-seed in my pocket."

A manuscript of the time of Elizabeth says:

> " Gather fearne seed on midsummer eve and
> Weare it about thee continually."

It would, as we said in enumerating magical stones, take up too much space in this essay to go through even half of the plants, herbs and trees considered in past days to have possessed occult powers. We will therefore only mention one tree whose leaves, dried and carried about as a talisman, had a very great vogue. We refer to the rowan. In England, Sweden and Holland it was looked on as the most potent instrument against the darker powers. Till recently, in out-of-the-way parts of Scotland (it may still be so), the Highlanders inserted crosses made of it with red thread in the lining of their clothes, the Cornish peasants carrying the same in their pockets and winding it round the horns of their cattle to keep off the Evil Eye. In Lancashire sprigs of it are still found hung up at bed-heads, and the churning staff generally made of its wood. In old days it used to stand in nearly every churchyard in Wales, and crosses of it were regularly distributed on the Church's festivals as sure preservatives against evil spirits. This no doubt was derived from the ancient Norsemen, who always used some of the wood of the rowan tree in their ships to secure them against storms, in whose mythology this tree was called Thor's Helper because it bent to his grasp in his passage over a flooded river on his way to the land of the Frost Giants.

What shall we say after this inquiry into all these strange things—scripts, stones, herbs and leaves our forefathers so used, and so thoroughly vouched the efficacy of? The answer seems to be that those magical objects filled a void in their nature which otherwise it would in vain have yearned for. If their faith had been stronger no such would have been wanted. If they had kept to that most excellent advice given in one of the ordinances of Philip the Fair of France for his soldiers to cast such aside and rely only on God, their good Right, their good horse and their arms, certainly as far as the military in the Middle Ages were concerned, they would have sought no further for these magical talismans and amulets. Alas! they had not all of them this stalwart faith, not to speak of the ordinary uneducated labouring classes or the higher ones among the nobility and princes; on the other hand there is little doubt, as these charmed articles were believed in, that they did in moments of danger on land and sea brace, by men's faith in them, their hearts and hands to face life's perils, for " so be it done unto thee according to thy faith " a greater than Solomon has said. If this be true, we need then seek no further to find, not in the articles of magic, but in the owner's and bearer's faith in them, their power and efficacy.

RUNNING THE MOLTEN METAL, PART OF
THE BELL FOUNDERS' WINDOW IN YORK
CATHEDRAL.

*Reproduced by permission from J. J. Raven's " The Bells of
England." (Methuen).*

ENGLISH BELLS

I DO not know anything that moves the heart more, on return to this fair country from foreign lands, than the English bells. To the exile abroad the remembrance of them is fragrant with sweet associations. To the soldier on the battlefield, to the sailor on the sea, to the traveller through the Great Desert, nothing is so redolent of the old country than to hear, in memory, those sweet-voiced bells of his homeland. They bring before him the old grey church, where as a child he prayed, and again he hears the sweet songs of the Christmas dawn interpreted through the old bells, and a man, possibly weary and worn when he finds them again on his return, no longer in memory but in reality, is moved to tears by their music. I mean not the mechanically constructed carillon, but the peal of old bells rung by the stalwart sunburnt peasant lad's strong arm, whose heart and soul, bred up in her fields, is full of love of England, and whose loyalty of heart is like the music of the bells, alike for old England.

Bells, it may be observed, belong to the most primitive class of musical instruments, those of percussion. Before nerve or sinew, stretched from point to point, had given forth their enlivening chords, before the reed with the pith extracted from it had

responded to the breath of human lungs, the clink of
chipped stone had made happy the pre-historic man, so
bells are but the children of those bits and ends of
stone, tin and copper, which the early cave-dwellers
looked on as pretty stones that gave forth sounds when
struck.

Bells have a very long pedigree.   In the Bible we
read of a golden bell and pomegranate on the robe of
the High Priest.   The Feast of Osiris certainly was
announced by the ringing of bells in Ancient Egypt.
Bells were employed in the religious rites of Cybele in
Athens and in the camp and garrisons of Greece.   All
these ancient bells were hand-bells.

Paulinus, Bishop of Nola, is generally credited to
have introduced them into Christian Churches.   These
hand-bells were made of thin plates of hammered iron,
wedge-shaped ; some of the Irish ones enclosed in
costly cases with designs in relief and enamel.   In
945 the Abbot of Croyland presented to that Abbey
a great bell which was the first tuneable one known.
His successor, Egelric, added six others.   Among the
bells was one named Bartholomew, that saint being
believed to have a power against thunder and lightning,
and in the Abbey it was said the relic of the identical
thumb which in his lifetime that saint used to cross
himself with in a storm, was kept.   All these ancient
bells were much longer and narrower than modern
ones.

There is every reason for believing that the art of
bell-founding, like the arts generally, was chiefly, if
not entirely, carried out under the direction of eccles-

iastics prior to the thirteenth century. When roads were bad and locomotion difficult, bells were frequently cast within the precincts of religious houses and in churchyards, which being cast the clergy or monks stood round and recited prayers and psalms. An instance of this occurred at St. Albans in the early part of the fourteenth century, when the great bell of the abbey called "Amphibalus," being broken, was re-cast in the hall of the sacristy. So, later, "Great Tom " of Lincoln, in 1610, was re-cast in the Minster yard. So, too, at Huddenham in the Isle of Ely, bells were cast within the walls of the Church.

Towards the close of that century, however, we find Roger de Ropeford of Paignton casting in 1284 four bells for the north tower of Exeter Cathedral. And Michael de Lichfield doing the same as a bell-founder in Lichfield. The so-called "Bell-founder " window in York Minster introduces us to Richard Tunnor as a bell-founder. He was Bailiff of York in 1320-1.

As bells cast in the thirteenth and fourteenth centuries were very rarely dated, it is difficult to point to many examples. A few are known. At present the oldest known dated bell in England hangs in St. Chad's Church, Claughton, Lancashire; it is dated 1296.

Change-ringing being unknown in pre-Reformation times, the founders of bells strove to produce grandeur and dignity rather than musical sequence in their bells. They effected this by using more metal in their casting.

With regard to the number of bells in the Middle Ages usual in Parish Churches, it may be said that whilst it seldom exceeded four, the miserable single bell, now so often heard, was almost unknown. Sometimes two are mentioned in the Edwardian's Returns of Church Goods, very rarely less than three.

Their Consecration.—Bells were, after being cast, set apart for holy purposes by a solemn benediction, so closely, to the ignorant, like the Office of Holy Baptism, that the ceremony often got called " The Baptism of the Bells."

This Office can be found in all the Medieval Pontificals, and varied very little after the ninth century.

The bell itself was washed by the bishop with water into which salt had previously been cast. After it had been dried by the acolytes, the bishop then dipped the thumb of his right hand in the holy oil for the sick, and made the sign of the Cross on the top of the bell; after which he again marked it both with the holy oil for the sick and with chrism, saying these words:

" Sancti + ficetur, et conse + cretur, Domine, signum istud; in nomine Pa + tris et Fi + lii, et Spiritus + sancti; in honorem Sancti N, pax tibi." After which the bell was censed.

Alcuin in the eighth century says, " Neque novum videri debet campanas benedicere et ungere eisque nomen imponere."

And in the Sarum " Manuale " in the Office of

consecrating bells, two sponsors for the bells are ordered.

Sometimes Indulgences were granted at the consecration of bells. Such was the case at Gamlingay, Cambridgeshire, where in 1490, John, Bishop of Ely, blessed a large bell in " honour of the Holy Ghost, and St. Nicholas the Confessor, and granted forty days indulgence to all those truly penitent, who should say, when they heard the sound of the great bell, five Paternosters and five Hail Mary's for the good of the Church, for the Bishop, the King, the Queen, and all the faithful Departed, adding, ' God have mercy on John, Bishop of Ely, that hallowed the altars and bells aforesaid, either sitting, standing, lying or kneeling.' "

The inscriptions on bells are so numerous, in fact few bells are without one, that it would be impossible in this essay to do more than touch on them—sufficient to give a few examples both of those before the Reformation (and so the older ones) and those after it. It will be observed that with pre-Reformation ones the usual inscription is the appeal to a Saint to pray for the people, the post-Reformation to leave this prayer out and to name them chiefly with a religious phrase or with secular names.

Whether it be superstitious or not, it cannot be denied there is something of romance in this prayer to the Saints being tossed upwards to heaven from many an old steepled church, and all through the dark nights of storm and stress, for some hamlet at its feet. St. Michael was thus frequently entreated to pray, his name carved on many an old bell, for was he not the powerful archangel who had worsted of old the power of Evil? Now our forefathers firmly believed storms and tempest were raised by the evil spirits; it was meet therefore that Michael, the conquerer of such in days long gone, should oppose them as they flew in the dark clouds of a storm to bring evil on a helpless land.

So, too, we find the other archangel's name often inscribed—Gabriel, whom our ancestors thought hunted with his pack of ghostly hounds the spirits of the dead on Hallow E'en; he therefore, too, seemed to them a suitable one to have his name and prayers asked on the storm-bell in the church tower.

Again, St. Catherine, because her legend was that she suffered martyrdom on a wheel, seemed a suitable saint—remembering the wheel the bells were suspended from—to intercede for the village and town. All such inscriptions we find on bells of pre-Reformation times. And as we remarked, whether a superstition or not, we can well conceive how comforting on a dark or stormy night it was to our ancestors, in many a hamlet or war-worn town, to feel thrown up to the gate of heaven, these appeals to powerful intercessors in these bell-waves of prayer.

Here is an ancient inscription invoking Gabriel at Althorpe, Lincolnshire: "*Missi de Cœlis nome Gabrielis.*" Here one invoking St. Oswald at Luddington, Lincoln: "See Oswalde *ora pro nobis.*" Here one invoking the Blessed Virgin at Thornton in Craven: "*Ave gra plena dns tecum.*" Another invoking the Baptist: "*See Johes Baptiste ora pro nobis, John Pudsey milite et Maria Consorte sue.*" On the second bell of Crosworth, Somerset, a dedication to St. Catherine: "*Hac Campanella colitur Katerina puella.*" On the second bell of Taddington, Derbyshire, to St. Michael: "*Custor sanctus nostrorum, Michael it dux animavinu.*"

These are a few pre-Reformation ones—the post-Reformation are left without invocations. For instance at Sempringham, Lincoln: "Be not over busie." At Pottersbury, Northants: "Prayes the Lord," 1625. At Foston, Lincoln: "Feare ye the Lord," 1658. At Wappenham, Northants: "God save King James," 1603. At Whitton, Northants, 1777: "Monarchy without tyranny."

And so far had any religious significance ceased on bells in the eighteenth century that we find in 1707 the names given to those in St. Helen's Church, Worcester, were: "Blenheim, Ramillies, Barcelona, Menin, Turin, Eugene, Marlborough, Queen Anne."

We all know as children the rhyme of St. Clements, in which the London city churches are enumerated. It is curious as giving expression to what people thought the bells said, as if living things, that other places also had these interpretations of bell-language. We find such at Northampton:

> " You owe me a shilling,
> Say the bells of Great Billing.
> When will you pay me?
> Say the bells of Middleton Cheney.

G

When I am able,
Say the bells of Dunstable.
That will never be,
Say the bells of Coventry.
O, yes, it will,
Says Northampton Great Bell.
White bread and sop,
Say the bells of Kingsthorpe.
Trundle a lantern,
Say the bells of Northampton.
Roast beef and marsh-mallows,
Say the bells of All Hallows.
Pancakes and fritters,
Say the bells of St. Peter's.
Roast beef and boiled,
Say the bells of St. Giles.
Poker and tongs,
Say the bells of St. John's (hospital).
Shovel, tongs and poker,
Say the bells of St. (Se)pulchres."

The whole alphabet, or a portion of it, is not infrequently met with as a bell inscription from the fourteenth or fifteenth to the seventeenth century. The letters are often in reversed order or otherwise misplaced. Encaustic tiles with the alphabet are also found, and even a christening bowl. Among other places where alphabet bells are found may be mentioned Bemerton, Wilts; Patrington, York; Leighton-Broomswould, Herts, which has three alphabet bells.

Here a short notice of the Curfew bell may be made. It still, after centuries of observance, is found in many places in England. The accepted origin is that it was instituted by the Conqueror in 1058, either to close the Saxons' beer-houses when at end of a day's work they there congregated and spoke treason against his rule, or to endeavour, by ordering all lights to be put out, to stay the often disastrous fires that took place from them being upset and kindling the thatched-roof dwellings.

This Curfew bell, however, before his time was well known on the Continent. Its repeal was made in the first year of Henry I—why, is not known, but its practice has remained through the ages, and its time when rung has varied in different places. In the Middle Ages it was not rung on Festival days, from the fact all the bells on those occasions were rung, and in the minds of the then Catholic population, it would become mixed up with the bell calling them to Vespers.

Small Bells were very frequent in the earliest days of Christianity. A small bell is said to have been presented to St. Teilo by the Patriarch of Jerusalem. The purposes of these small bells were many, and to assemble the people the early missionary would carry one about with him. Giraldus Cambrensis tells us "both laity and clergy in Ireland, Scotland and Wales (and it is probable a like belief was current in England) held in such veneration certain portable bells that they were more afraid of swearing falsely by them than by the Gospels because of some miraculous and hidden power with which they were gifted, and by the vengeance of the saint to whom they were particularly pleasing, their despisers and transgressors were severely punished."

Wynkyn de Worde, printer of "The Golden Legend," observes: "It is said that spirytes that ben in the region of th' ayre doubte moche when they here the belles ringen whan it thunderth, and when grete tempeste and rages of wether happen, to the ende that the feinds and wycked spirytes should ben abashed and flee and cease of the movynge of tempeste."

In a representation of the funeral procession of Edward the Confessor, on the Bayeaux tapestry, two boys are depicted as ringing two hand-bells. In the inventory of the goods of the Church of Sherburn-in-Elmet, in the early part of the tenth century, preserved at York, four hand-bells are mentioned.

It is no wonder, therefore, in old days a proper bell-man—or else an acolyte as now in Latin countries—often preceded a funeral procession ringing a little hand-bell. Thus in Floresta's "Espanola" (p. 123) we read: "De Ayala went away to the Court Brotherhood and requested them to bring one who had died at the Marquis's, and then away to the funeral procession with the little death-bell tinkling before them." Mackenzie Walcott mentions about 1855 two cases of a bell-man with his little bell preceding the funerals at Oxford of two undergraduates. Formerly, too, according to a very ancient custom on the night preceding the execution of condemned criminals the bell-man of St. Sepulchre's Church, London, went under Newgate and rang his little bell—called the death-bell, at the same time giving the condemned a versified little sermon ending up with—"And when St. Sepulchre's bell to-morrow tolls, the Lord have mercy on your souls. Past twelve o'clock! "

When a priest in this country, as still in certain foreign ones, carried the Host through the streets to the sick, a hand-bell was rung before him. It was the custom to muffle this bell while in the sick chamber, as we find in an illumination in Clifford's Pontifical. (Corpus Christi College, Cambridge.)

So the practice of perambulating a town with one bell or more, after a death, or at a funeral, or year-day, was very general. Thus we find in a will of a certain John Baret he bequeaths his house to the priest of St. Mary's Church with other provisos, on condition that he arranged for his father and mother and his own soul a procession should take place when " the bellemeen " were to have " iij " for their service. But the present practice of ringing little bells in tune in octaves, cannot be traced, even as near the Stuart period; it is quite a recent invention.

Sacrament Bell.—This was different to the small bell used in the Mass at the Elevation; it seemed used to advertise the villages of the Mass about to commence, or after the Reformation to advertise the pause between Morning Prayer and the Communion Office. Thus Bishop Hooper in his " Articles of Visitation " asks, " In case there be any pause between the Morning Prayer and Communion then in order to advertise and signify unto the people—to toll one bell." We find this practice still at several places, e.g., at All Saints, Holbeach, this bell is rung at the end of the Litany, and St. Peter-in-Eastgate, Lincoln,

and Winterton, Lincolnshire, the treble bell is used
to be rung at the end of the sermon.

It seems extremely likely the little " squint
windows " in many of our country churches, popularly
called leper windows, and thought for a long time to
be for the convenience of persons afflicted with leprosy
to view the Mass, were not windows provided for that
purpose but for the server in church to ring this
Sacrament Bell that non-attendants in the village
might know what period of the service was reached, or
else for the ringing of the holier little bell—the
" Sacring Bell," used at the Elevation of the Host.

The reason why many archæologists have come to
the conclusion these little windows in these churches
were probably used for ringing a bell from within the
church so that those outside might hear, and not for
the use of leprosy-stricken folk to look through and
see the Mass progressing, is that no person was
allowed to be about or mingle with his fellows in those
ages stricken with leprosy, but were always isolated
from the hale and hearty, and certainly would not
therefore have been allowed to be in the churchyards
when the congregation came to and out of the church.

Sometimes in these times, instead of the small bell,
one or more of the larger bells were used at the
Elevation. In Archbishop Peckham's Constitutions
at Lambeth we read, " Wherefore let them (the
parishioners) be first warned by ringing the little bell,
and at the Elevation let the great bell be thrice
knolled."

So later, in 1471, " At the Elevation of the Host

both the greater and the less one of the greater bells shall henceforth be tolled for a while."

Sometimes this Sacring Bell was hung at the door of the nave; sometimes hung from the rood-loft. An existing example is still at Salhouse, Norfolk; it was sometimes described as one little bell hanging in the church called the Saints Bell. (Reliquary XI, 231.)

Sometimes a number of small bells affixed to a wheel, which, pulled by a cord, gave warning for the Elevation.

This Sacring Bell was sometimes called "The Agnus Bell," as it was followed immediately after the Elevation by the singing of the Agnus Dei; so it was called as an instance of this at Hemswell, Lincolnshire. (Peacock's "Church Furniture," p. 103.)

In the Lay-folks Mass-book, 1375, the use of the Sacring Bell is referred to as a well-known custom:

> " A litel belle men oyse to ryng
> Hen shall hon do renerence
> To ihesu crist awen presence."

And Lydgate, born in 1370, says of himself in his boyhood:

> " Rediere chirstoonys (cheery stones) for to telle
> Than gon to chirche or heere the sacry belle."

These little bells, whether rung by hand for accompanying the Host to the sick, or at funerals, or in calling men's minds to the devouter part of a Church service, were often carved on "Misereres" by medieval artisans, and even parodied. Thus in one of the windows of York Minster is a satire on the Yorkshireman's love of funerals, and interesting as it shows the bell carried at such. A monkey is being carried to rest by other monkeys. In front of the bier are a monkey bell-ringer and a monkey carrying the processional cross. The monkey widow weeps, but the monkey-undertaker consumes cake and wine with great relish!

The Passing Bell.—This is peculiar to England, and one of the earliest recorded uses to which the church bell was put. Bede mentions it (Bede, Book IV, c. XXIII) as the " well-known sound of the bell which they (the nuns of Hackness) were wont to be roused or assembled to prayer, when any one of them was called forth from this world." It was heard, he says too, on the death of St. Hilda of Whitby, in 680.

Durandus, who wrote about the end of the twelfth century, says, " When anyone is dying, bells must be tolled that the people may put up their prayers —twice for a woman and thrice for a man; if for an ecclesiastic, as many times as he had orders." Even after the Reformation this bell was spared. It was then usual to ring or toll the Passing Bell while the person was dying, but not yet dead. So the Protestant Grindal ordered it so to be used, " To move the people to pray for sick person "; so, too, the sixty-seventh canon of the Anglican Church provides that " when anyone is passing out of this life a bell shall be tolled, and the minister shall not then be slack to do his last duty."

Shakespeare refers to this bell in Henry IV:

" Yet the first bringer of unwelcome news
Hath but a losing office; and his tongue
Sounds ever after as a sullen bell
Remember'd knolling a departed friend."

This Passing Bell was in past times tolled at all hours of the day and night, whenever, that is, a sick person lay in his or her last extremity.

We can fancy to those waking up in the depth of a dark winter night and hearing this bell, how their own mortality must have dawned on them, and how weird this deep bell beseeching their prayers must have struck them.

We find many instances of fees paid for such death-bells—thus at Exeter at the Cathedral in 1670, is noted down in the accounts, " For tolling the bell for every sick person, 1/-. For every child, 6d." At Barrow-on-Humber among the clerk's fees in 1713, " For every passing bell four pence, and for every soul bell four pence."

About this time the old custom gave way through the country at large, and the modern custom came in of ringing the bell only *after* the death.

At the close or commencement, or at both, of the Passing Bell, it has long been the custom—as before has been said—to denote the sex of the person departed by certain strokes of the bell. Three for a male, in honour of the Blessed Trinity. Two for a woman, in honour of our Saviour born of a woman, and this on the tenor bell. But these tolls very much differ in different places. An able writer on the subject states that in Lincolnshire alone the different ways of ringing the Passing Bell are upwards of seventy in number.

The inscriptions on some of these tenor bells refer to their use as a Passing Bell. Thus at Whitechurch, Hampshire:

" ,When I toll
The Lord save the soul."

So at Strathern, Leicestershire:

" My roaring sounde doth warning give
That men cannot heare always lyve."

So in another church in the same county:

" When you die,
Aloud I cry."

At Hambledon, Rutland, is an inscription which refers to the modern custom in contrast with the ancient:

"Non sono animabus mortuorum sed auribus viventium."

Under the Penal Laws, when all services of the old Faith were forbidden and such held only in secrecy, no bells were used, of course, and even now, though members, not of the Church of England, are, by law, if parishioners, permitted to be buried in her churchyards, no Passing Bell is allowed to be tolled. However, a writer in " Notes and Queries " (Vol. II, 1850) writes: " It is currently reported in Yorkshire that three curious privileges belong to the head of the ancient Catholic family of Vuvasour of Haslewood: (1) That he may ride on horseback into York Minster.

(2) That he may specially call his house a Castle.
(3) That he may toll a bell in his chapel notwithstanding any law prohibiting the use of bells not in
communion with the Church of England."

A curious custom in some scattered parishes in
England has been to toll the bell while the congregation has been leaving the church. It seems to have
arisen to inform those who had not attended the
morning service there would be another in the after-
noon. Or it has been suggested it might be rung to
tell all stay-at-home housewives, as a warning to get
ready the mid-day dinner! Such a custom has been
found at Crawley, Winchester and Tytherley, and
at Bray, Maidenhead and Olney. Another solution
of this custom offered is to give notice to any funeral
procession that the ordinary service was over, and the
Church free to conduct that of the funeral, which often
is arranged for on Sundays in out-of-the-way parishes.

A curious incident is handed down of a man who
endeavoured to raise money to provide money
available to erect a peal of bells at Whiston Church,
Northants. Anthony Catesby, the man in question,
had spent so much in erecting the church, he found
to his sorrow he had none for the bells. He therefore
sold his flock of sheep, and when he heard the sound
of the bells coming over the valley of the Nene to
Ecton, where he dwelt with his wife, he said to her,
" Hark! Do ye hear my lambs bleating? " He died
in 1553. (" Church Bells," by T. North, F.S.A.)

A very curious bequest among other bequests for
bells to be rung at funerals and anniversaries of

deaths, was that of Thomas Nash of Bath to the ringers of the Abbey there. He bequeathed £50 a year to such on condition they rang, on the day he had been married, a solemn and doleful peal of bells, muffled, from eight o'clock in the morning till eight o'clock at night; secondly, on the day he died a joyful peal in commemoration of his happy release from domestic tyranny and wretchedness!

Many bequests were in old days left for the endowment of bells to be rung at night, directing belated wayfarers; thus the bells, out of many instances, at Langham, Rutland, had money left for the future ringing of the bells because to a lady once benighted they directed her home.

The writer of " Church Bells of Shropshire " records a ringing custom at Wentnor annually on Church Stretton Fair Day, in memory of a man called Smith, of Wentnor, who lost his way crossing the Longmynd. His family left an annual sum for the ringers in order that the bells rung might guide other such travellers.

Perhaps the most romantic legends of bells are those which, by shipwreck or by being submerged in the sea, are still heard ringing. Such are the bells of Boscastle. In old days the inhabitants resolved to have a peal of bells in the neighbouring village of Forrabury. The bells were shipped, the bells were blessed. The pilot thanked God on his knees as he drew near port, for their safety. The captain jeered at his piety and swore. A sudden wave came thereupon rolling down, engulfing the barque and its cargo of bells. As the ship sank the bells were heard tolling with a muffled peal, and ever since then the bells of Forrabury are heard to listening and startled ears tolling beneath the waves, and the tower of Forrabury has never had its bells.

> " Still when the storm of Bottreau's waves
> Is waking in his weedy caves,
> Those bells that sullen surges hide
> Peal their deep notes upon the tide—
> ' Come to thy God in time! '
> Thus saith the ocean chime;
> ' Storm, billow, whirlwind past,
> Come to thy God at last.' "

Romantic narratives about stolen or submerged bells are numerous. It is reasonably so, for the natives in remote hamlets, particularly those by storm-beaten and wrecked shores, would associate these bells in the belfries as something more than human; hung, as it were, between heaven and earth, their voices and no others are carried over the restless sea—to warn, to welcome, and to guide.

In Jersey, all its twelve churches are credited with beautiful and valuable rings of bells. It was afore-time decided to gather these together and sell them for war expenses and ship them to France for that purpose. The ship with them foundered and the bells went to the bottom. To this day, it is said, when a storm is blowing up, their sound comes from the depths of the sea, and the fishermen of St. Ouen's Bay always therefore go down to the beach before starting out, to

hear if "the bells upon the wind" sound or not.
(Raven's "Bells of England.")

> " 'Tis an omen of death to the mariner
>   Who wearily fights with the sea,
>   For the foaming surge is his winding sheet
>   And his funeral knell are we—
>   His funeral knell our passing bell
>   And his winding sheet the sea."

Again, there are other bells on land which are said
to have rung *of themselves* at a death.   The Lincoln
Minster bells are said to have been heard on the night
of the great Bishop Crosseteste's death, by Basset,
Bishop of London, who happened to be near the
country residence of the Lincoln bishop on the night
of his departure in 1253; so, at least, Matthew Paris
in his Chronicle tells us.   Then at Lincoln itself was
a similar manifestation of bells invisibly ringing at the
burial of the child-martyr Hugh when—

> " A' the bells of merrie Lincoln
>   Without men's hands were rung;
>   And a' the books of merrie Lincoln
>   Were read without men's tongue;
>   And ne'er was such a burial
>   Sin' Adam's days begun."

Now how shall we end this little essay on our dear
English bells?   It can be with no "bidding prayer"
in some old College Chapel recounting ancient
worthies—but the chapel of the bells shall be the sky
at eventide when their voice shall ring out with

"Gloria in excelsis Deo," and their epitaph shall be when they ring the last Curfew, like this:

> "I love ye chimes of Motherland
>   With all this soul of mine,
> And bless the Lord that I am sprung
>   Of good old English line.
> And like a son I sing the lay
>   That England's glory tells;
> For she is lovely to the Lord,
>   For you, ye Christian Bells."

CAROLS AND THEIR ENVIRONMENT

THE writer thinks, in these heavily taxed days, many like himself have found old families driven out of their estates, living in small and modern houses. But from a love of those ancestral homes and their associations, such have brought with them into their modern dwellings much of their old china, old furniture and old pictures. What is the effect of such? A discordance, a want of harmony. Torn from those ancient walls, the pictures look homeless, the old china no longer beautiful; old things, in a word, require old surroundings to be beautiful.

Feeling this to be true also of old carols, the writer has endeavoured in this essay, by placing them in a setting of old customs, to preserve the beauty of several: so best can they be appreciated. Is there not a similar case in that of the old Border Ballads, so full of true pathos and charm? Yes, but not read in a great modern town, but read on the open moor, on the purple heather of the north, beside the rushing Solway, as it was once crossed by the wild moss-trooper, in those passionate days when a woman would say:

" I'll tak the red gold frae my hair
And follow thee for ever mair! "

There are a great many old customs of Christmas which, now observed, would be looked on as superstitious or ridiculous; there are others which, if practised nowadays, would fail to work any impression on the people—because the " atmosphere " they had about them in the days of old has departed; and there are others died out because, particularly in the villages and countrysides, the whole feeling of the peasantry to their lords has worn threadbare or from a change of ownership is no longer practised.

As has just been remarked, perhaps of all the reasons why these old customs and the social side of Christmas has deteriorated, is the want of the " atmosphere " which once surrounded them. The want of this makes nowadays the social observances of the season so often wearisome to simulate, that many people weary at keeping up such a pretence, and are glad when Christmas is over.

Now that " atmosphere," whether founded on superstition or on some forgotten realities, or some long-lost power in the soul of man, was a *belief in the unseen world around;* the close connection with mankind of others whose unseen presence awed, if it did not dignify, all their holidays and working days; and Christmas was no exception in the participation of such beings.

To sit by the Yule log, to dance in the old raftered hall and know by that hearth and dancing by their sides in the hall a fairy throng too were there, certainly gave our forefathers something which we in our Christmas revels lack.

So on All Souls' Eve to look out at midnight on the sky and believe in seeing Gabriel with his hounds

H

chasing the souls of the dead, or the Wild Hunter chasing them over moor and field until cock-crow, certainly gave that strange Night of the Dead an atmosphere which carried weight and faith to the onlookers, which we at the present day on that Eve lack. And so many of the observances of Christmas, even many of its festal dishes, linked by name or belief to the unseen dwellers round mankind, brought with them an atmosphere we in this matter-of-fact and prosaic age find wanting in our Christmasses; we may grant they were but gilt, yet they were the gilt on our gingerbread, and made the gingerbread sweet.

The belief in the "Little Folk," as the fairies were named, was almost universal with our ancestors. At Christmas, outside their doors, some portion of food was left for these little ones, on each platter on which the circle round the fire ate their Christmas dinner. The writer remembers, even so late as his own childhood, his nurses telling him this, and unconsciously still, years after, he frequently finds himself doing so. It was little wonder such a belief, then universal, that those of lang syne heard in the snow-covered forest on Christmas night elfin music, and traced on the snow the rings of fairy feet, or a lad, opening his lattice at midnight, heard:

> " Come frolick youth and follow me,
>   My beauteous boy, and I'll show thee
>   The country of the Fairie."
>   —*Drayton.*

This belief gave a mystery and a strange and secret joy to the reveller in farm and hall, and one feels inclined to echo Voltaire's words—when all these beliefs have for ever gone from us—

> " O l'heureux temps que celui de ses fables
> Des bons démons, des esprits familiers,
> Des forfadets aux mortels secourables!
> On écoutait tous ces faits admirables
> Dans son château, près d'un large foyer:
> Ouvraient l'oreille à Monsieur l'aumônier,
> Qui leur ferait des contes de sorcier.
> On a banni les démons et les fées."

Perhaps, as has been suggested by some writers who have made popular antiquities their peculiar study, all fairy mythology may be referred to a confused tradition of a primeval race of men, who were gradually driven out by the encroachments of more advanced civilization. According to this theory, the inferior race retired into the most remote parts of woods and hills, and gradually these inferior and smaller races became in popular estimation a fairy folk. Thus universal belief in a Fairy Race was held so firmly by our far-off ancestors.

Closely allied to these Forest Folk was the Yule log, which at Christmas, with much ceremony, was introduced into hall and cottage. Our ancestors, despite their being Christians, imperceptibly derived from their pagan Norse countrymen reverence for trees.

The word " Yule," and so the log of wood thus named, seems to have come from the Celtic word " Hiaul," or " Houl," which signifies the sun. It was a common custom that everywhere prevailed among the Celts, to celebrate a feast of the winter solstice when they saw the sun return again to the heavens. This was their greatest solemnity of the year; hence when the Christian feast of Christmas was fixed at the winter solstice, the sun-log, or Yule log, survived.

Another derivation is that the word " Yule " stands for " Jol," which means a wheel or revolution, typifying the revolution of the sun in the heavens. Both derivations show the remains of ancient sun worship, the log itself, round in shape, being the symbol of that great solar luminary. At all events, with great rejoicing all through our forefathers' time, the great Yule log at Christmas was brought to their hearths, with song, and dancing, and merriment. It was, indeed, the advance guard of Christmas. Such, too, not only provided warmth in the draughty houses at Christmas, but its glowing embers took the place of modern lighting. Torches were burnt, and, later, tallow candles with wicks of rush; but the great hearth, with the enormous log of wood burning night and day, was far more effective. Even in the towns the Yule log was cherished. In the northern parts of the country, after service on Christmas Day, the people, even in the churches, cried " Ule, ule," as a token of rejoicing, and the lads ran about the streets singing:

> " Ule, ule, ule, ule,
> Three puddings in a pule,
> Crack nuts and cry Ule,"

while a rather stingy proverb ran: " It is good to cry ' Ule ' at other men's costs."

As we are on the subject of trees and their logs,

it may be as well to make some reference to a very prevalent custom still in vogue among us—the Christmas tree. The introduction of this to our own country has generally been ascribed to the late German Prince Albert. He, like the other German princes, no doubt popularized it, for they derived from their Teuton ancestors a reverence for trees. Yet as far back as the time of Henry VIII we find in the description of a pageant a tree to have been a prominent feature:

"Agaynst the XIIth daye, or the daye of the Epiphanie, at nighte before the banket in the hall at Richmonde was a pageaunt devised like mountayne glysteringe by nighte at the top of whiche mountayne was a tree of golde, the braunches and leaves frysed with golde spredynge on every side over the mountayne with roses and pomegarnettes."

Still a tree decorated at Christmas in later times without doubt came from Germany. A writer in "Notes and Queries" says: "We remember a German of the household of the late Queen Caroline making what he termed a Christmas tree for a child's party at this festive season."

An old writer observes of trees: "Twice they have acted in man's salvation—i.e., by saving him in the Ark, and later by the Cross."

We have here dealt with inanimate objects. Now we will touch on songs sung by boys and men at Christmas time called "carols." The word "carol" in its derivation has been debated. Some ascribe it to the word "chorus," but others, more reasonably, to the debased Latin word "corolla"—a small crown or ring; for the ancient way of singing carols was singing them when dancing in a ring.

That the word "carol" seems to have been a word for ring, or circle, is borne out by the fact that in old days the group, or ring, of stones at Stonehenge was called the "Carol." At all events, though songs sung while dancing were originally derived from pagan worship at an early period, they penetrated into the Christian. The third Council of Toledo (589) acknowledged the custom, but only restrained such dancing and singing in the churches on the Vigils of Saints' Days, and a later Provincial Council at Avignon, in 1207, forbade theatrical dances and secular songs in churches. Probably the only surviving religious dance in a church is that which still obtains in the Cathedral at Seville and Echternach in Luxembourg. To a late date Morris dancing in this country certainly obtained in the naves of some of our churches. The accounts of St. Mary's, Reading, as late as 1556-7 contain entries of the wardens for the necessary dresses and properties for such in the church. John Aubrey says that in his day Yorkshire folk danced in the churches at Christmas. One of the old Morris dances performed in a church was called "Bean-setting," derived probably from a primitive ceremonial dance which was once performed in the springtime when the crops were sown. (See Johnson's "Bye-ways in British Archæology," p. 185.)

However, there is little doubt that the church edifice originally was where the earliest Christian carols were sung or danced, and that they were developments out of the Latin festival hymns.

The verse of a carol is very often at first moulded upon the form of these hymns in time of four or three beats alternately. In all probability both were written by ecclesiastics, the carols representing an attempt to bring the meaning of Christmas nearer home to the people. Indeed the French author, the Abbé Arnaud, asserts this permission to sing carols and, in churches in the vulgar tongue, was for that purpose allowed by the Bishops: " Les évêques par une condescendance aussi paternelle qu'éclairée, permirent que cette innovation, imposée par le malheur des temps " (i.e., from the gradual disuse of the Latin tongue by the common people).

This contest, if we may call it so, between the ecclesiastical Latin and the vernacular, can well be seen in the well-known Boar's Head carol, the solo of which is in English, the chorus in Latin, while the last line of the solo is also in the Latin tongue. This mingling of the more sonorous and stately Latin, either as interposed in separate verses or sung as a chorus, as in many carols, has a beautiful and fine effect. Whether ecclesiastics were chiefly responsible for the old carols as authors, or the lay folk for some. all the authors adapted their themes suitable to the spirit and capacity of the singers. In those days religion and secular life so overlapped that to introduce the events, persons and characters of the one into the other was to these simple people no mark of irreverence. As a landscape painter puts in his picture all the still life he sees in his prospect, so the villagers who composed or sung these carols put into them what daily they saw happening round them. Seeing the oxen in their fields daily yoked to the plough; seeing the ass bearing their bundles daily to market, relying on an old prophecy, they continually, in their sacred carols, introduced them into the stable of Bethlehem. Observing the care of their mothers at home and how they soothed their infants, with their ingenuous lullabies, they did not scruple, in their primitive souls, to make the Virgin-Mother send her Divine Child to sleep with the same lullabies: or seeing—if they dwelt by the sea-shore—three ships sailing away, they did not hesitate to give these ships a mystical meaning and introduce them into a sacred carol. In a word, the home life of their village, with all its common objects, they introduced into their carols with no feeling of irreverence towards the holier and more spiritual scenes of Bethlehem and Nazareth. In this French carol following, the birds and animals introduced into it as speeding each other to Bethlehem, were considered perfectly in the spirit we have just spoken of:

> " Comme les bestes autrefois
> Parloient mieux latin que françois,
> Le coq, de loin voyant le fait,
> S'écria : Christus natus est.
> Le bœuf d'un air tout ébaubi
> Demande : Ubi ? Ubi ? Ubi ?

> La chèvre, se tordant le groin
> Répond que c'est à Bethleem.
> Maistre Baudet, curiosus
> De l'aller voir, dit: Eamus;
> Et, droit sur ses patres, le veau
> Beugle deux fois: Volo, Volo! "

And if our forefathers then enlisted the birds and animals to glorify the stable at Bethlehem, they also recalled in the snows of winter some of the spring and summer flowers to garland their carols of the Holy Child. The following one is in the quaint spelling of Richard Hill, of the time of Elizabeth, whose very valuable manuscript Placebook of Carols is in the library of Balliol College, Oxford. In it the lily is the Holy Child.

> " Synge we alle for tyme it is
> Mary hath born ye flowre delice.[1]

> 1. For his love, that bowght us all dere
> Lystyn, lordyngis that ben here
> And I will tell you infere[2]
> Wher-of com ye flowr delyce.

> Synge we alle for tyme it is
> Mary hath born ye flowre delice.

> 2. On Christmas nyght, whan it was cold
> Our lady lay amonge bestis bolde
> And ther she bare Jhesu, Josepff tolde
> And ther com the flowr delice.

> Synge we alle for tyme it is
> Mary hath born ye flowre delice."

---

[1] *De lys*—lily.
[2] Together.

So another carol (*circa* 1426) entwines the Holy
Child with flowers:

" Angels came from out of their tower
 To look upon this freshly Flower;
 How fair He was in His colour,
 And how sweet in His savour
     And to behold
 How such a Flower might spring in gold!

 Of Lily, of rose, of ryse,[1]
 Of primrose and of fleur-de-lys,
 Of all the flowers at my device
 That Flower of Jesse yet bears the price
     As most of neal
 To slake our sorrows every deal.

 I pray thee flowers of this countree
 Wherever ye go, wherever ye be,
 Hold up the Flower of good Jesse
 For your freshness and your beauty,
     As fairest of all
 And ever was and ever shall."

Again, from seeing in many of their rude cottages
the mothers soothing to sleep by little songs their
babies, such in their minds being one of the most
touching things in their rustic and uneventful lives,
they wove it in many a carol while the lullabies still
rang in their ears.   Here is a verse of such a
carol:

---

[1] Branch.

" This enders[1] nyght
I sawe a sight
A sterre as bryght
As any day
And ever a-monge
A madyn songe
Lulley, by, by, lully, lulley!

1. A lovely lady sat and songe
And to her son thus gan she say
' My son, my lord, my dere derlyng
Why liggis thou thus in the hay?
My own dere son
How art thou cum
Art thou not God verey?
But none the lesse
I will not sces
To synge by, by; lully, lulley.' "

And the following excerpt from a carol of the Wise Men shows in the fourth verse how the spirit of chivalry was still ripe and the Holy Child was addressed as in " Knyght-hood ":

" Be mery all that be present
Omnes de Saba venient."

" 4. Forth they went by ye sterres leme[2]
Till they com to mery Bethlehem
Ther they fond that swet barn-teme[3]
That sith for us his blode hath spent.

5. Balthasar kneled first a down
And said ' Hayll Kyng, most of renown
And of all Kyngis thou berist ye crown
Therfor with gold I the present.'

---

[1] Enders—other.　　　　[2] Ray.　　　　[3] Child.

6. Melchior kneled down in that stede[1]
   And said ' Hayll, Lord, in thy pryest-hede
   Receyve ensence to thy man-hede
   I brynge it with a good entent.'

7. Jasper kneled down in that stede
   And said ' Hayll, Lord, in thy Knight-hede
   I offer the myrre to thy Godhede
   For thou art he that all hath sent.' "

This sentiment of the age of chivalry, looking on our Lord as a Knight, is still better exemplified by the following carol, sung before the year 1556, and probably of a much earlier date in its first form: it probably dates from 1400. " The Bleeding Knight " is Christ, the " May " is his Mother, the " falcon " is probably introduced as the ox and ass were in some of the other carols of the Nativity by the people (as mentioned before) to bring into the night of Christ's Birth, things and creatures they saw daily in their countryside:

" Lully, lulley, lully lulley,
The falcon hath borne my make[2] away.

He bare him up, he bare him down,
He bare him into an orchard brown.

In that orchard there was an hall
That was hanged with purple and pall.

And in that hall there was a bed,
It was ranged with gold so red.

And in that bed there lieth a Knight,
His wounds bleeding day and night.

---

[1] Spot.   [2] Maker.

By that bedside kneeleth a May,
And she weepeth both night and day.

And by that bedside standeth a stone,
' Corpus Christi ' written thereon."

Somewhat akin to carol music—as both are often performed in the streets—a brief notice should be made of those old-fashioned musicians who, not yet totally died out, parade our streets with very lugubrious music at Christmas, when most folks are in bed.   I mean the Waits.   The word " wait " is from the Anglo-Saxon " wacan," to wait or watch, and was very appropriate to these men, as originally they were the " watch " who paraded our streets at night under our Tudor and later kings.   These earliest watch, or waits, in the fourteenth and fifteenth centuries played sounding horns or even flageolets.   The Black Book of Edward IV provided for such a watch " to pipe the watching."   Rules in the same book are laid down: the watch is to eat in the hall with the minstrels, to sup off half a loaf and to have half a gallon of ale each. Certain towns also had regulated waits—such as Canterbury—and received a stipulated salary.

Till the beginning of the year 1800, the London waits used to have a special livery—blue gowns with red caps and sleeves.   Now they have come down to certain unrecognized old men, who at Christmas wake the early hours with their discordant instruments.

It may be of interest to add that the only watchmen officially recognized to call out the hours as they pass at night, still exist in the quaint little privileged enclosure of Ely Place.

In the enumeration of Christmas customs must not be forgotten the custom of decking the churches and private houses with green boughs. Stowe, in his survey of London, writes against the feast of Christmas: "All the houses, as well as the parish churches, were decked with holme (oak), ivy, bayes, etc. The conduits and standards in the streets were likewise garnished."

According to this old carol, holly was greatly preferred by our ancestors to the ivy. It runs:

" Nay nay Ive, it may not be iwis
    For holy must have ye mastry, as ye maner is
    Holy berith beris, beris rede ynowgh
    Y^e thristilcok, ye popyngay dance in euery bow(gh)
    Welaway, sory ivy, what fowles hast thow
    But ye sory howlet that syngith ' How, how '?
    Nay, nay Ive, it may not be iwis
    For holy must have ye mastry, as ye maner is.

    Holy and his mery men sytt in cheyres of gold:
    Ivy and her jentyll women sytt with-owt in fold
    With a payre of kybid helis cawght with cold
    So wold I that euery man had, that with Yvy will hold.
    Nay, nay Ive, it may not be iwis
    For holy must have ye mastry as ye maner is."
                        —From the Balliol MS. 354 of Richard Hill,
                            temp. Elizabeth.

In an ancient calendar of the Catholic Church we find the following observation on Christmas Eve: " Templa exornantur " (churches are decked). But among all this greenery, mistletoe was strictly forbidden to be brought into the churches owing to its long association in the past with the pagan worship of the Druids. If ever it was found in churches it was probably put there through ignorance. Mistletoe had been at the festival of the winter solstice conspicuous in that pagan cult, carried in the hands of their priests, and laid on their altars, and called by them " All Heal." However, though excluded from the churches, it was displayed in every manor hall and lower dwelling at Christmas. It was supposed to have a magical influence, hung up there with the charm attached to it that the maid who was not kissed under it at Christmas would not be married that year. (Nares.)

No doubt this use of decking churches and dwelling houses at Christmas was used by our forefathers as a symbol of the peace brought us by the birth of Christ and also of the victory He won later over death, both borrowed from the custom of the ancient Romans, who decked their houses, both public and private, with green laurels, and palms, and oak leaves, as symbols of peace and victories won. Indeed the more we examine into the old customs of Christmas, the more we find originally most of them spring from the pagan worship of the ancients; and as far as those introduced by our Saxon ancestors, remnants of Sun worship. It seems to have been indeed a wise procedure of the Christian Church, remembering, as she did, many of these old pagan customs were endeared by long usage to the nations she conquered and Christianized, instead of destroying these customs and usages, that she gave such a

Christian significance and sanctity and permitted them to remain.

Christmas Dancing. — Dances were proverbial during the Christmas season, whether in the manor house, or village ale-house, or humbler cottage; often, too, if weather permittted, they danced in the village street or cobbled town-road, and all were expected to contribute their talents to amuse. So this old carol of 1558 says:

> " Make we merry both more and less
> For now is the time of Christmas!
>
> Let no man come into the hall,
> Groom, page nor yet marshal,
> But that some sport he bring withal
>   For now is the time of Christmas!
>
> If that he say he cannot sing,
> Some other sport then let him bring
> That it may please at this feasting
>   For now is the time of Christmas!
>
> If he say he can naught do
> Then for my love ask him no mo'
> But to the stocks then let him go
>   For now is the time of Christmas! "

Between the dances there would be singing— either one of the semi-religious carols or else one such as follows, which we can imagine, when pressed to sing, some young rustic would give:

> " 1. I have XII oxen be fayre and brown
> And they go a grasynge down by the town
> With hay, wild howe, wild hay!
> Sawyste thou not myn oxen, you litill prety boy?

2. I have XII oxen and they be fayre and whight
   And they go a grasynge down by the dyke
   With hay, wild howe, wild hay!
   Sawyste thou not myn oxen, you litill prety boy?

3. I have XII oxen and they be fayre and blak
   And they go a grasynge down by the lak
   With hay, wild howe, with hay!
   Sawyste thou not myn oxen, you litill prety boy?

4. I have XII oxen and they be fayre and red
   And they go a grasynge down by the mede
   With hay, wild howe, with hay!
   Sawyste thou not myn oxen, you litill prety boy?"
   —From Richard Hall Collection *temp*. Elizabeth.

The deep snows (for seldom in the past was Christmas without its snow), the terrible roads, often only a pack-horse track from village to village, confined the population much indoors. Public amusements such as now, the cinema and cheap theatres, were unknown. Musicians, if at all, were wandering glee-men, or the three old men who in most village churches provided on Sundays, with their antique instruments, the only music. Folk in those days had to rely on themselves for amusements during the long dark evenings; and this led to an immense amount of dancing.

Country dances, so called not because they were danced in the country but from the "contre danse," i.e., lads standing in a row opposite the lassies, and so footing it—these prevailed everywhere. Even in royal palaces, where foreign dances had been imported, the country dance followed. Thus, at Christmas,

I

1622-3, we read : " The Prince Charles did lead the measures with the French Ambassador's wife. The measures—braules, corrantoes, and galliards being ended, the masquers with the ladies did dance two country staves." So again, when Charles II was king, at Whitehall, after dancing a corranto we read, " then to country dances, the king leading the first which he called for, which was, said he, ' Cuckolds all awry,' which was the old dance of England."

There is no doubt many of these old dances had songs sung by the performers to their measures. Baker, in his " Principles of Music," 1636, says: " In this kind is also comprehended the infinite multitude of ballads set to sundry pleasant and delightful tunes by cunning and witty composers with *country dances* fitted into them."

Our modern word " ballet " was derived from the word " ballad "—the old ballad sung by the dancers as they toed the floor; and it must have lent a charm to these rollicking old dances to hear from the voices of youth the rollicking old songs, making the rafters echo with joy and laughter, while outside the snow fell, and the winds whistled down the great open fireplaces upon the Yule log, and the father and mother sat by it and thought how they too in a long, long past Christmas had sung and danced as their children now were doing. We give here a few of some of the quaintest named of these country dances as danced by our great-grandfathers and grandmothers: " Buttered Pease "; " Have at thy coat, old woman "; " Bobbing Joan "; " The Dumps "; " Rub her down with a straw," or a more prettily named one—" Sweet Kate."

There was also both a country dance and a ballad tune set to it in the sixteenth and seventeenth centuries under the gruesome name, " Of the Doleful Dance and Song of Death," the tune also even called " The Shaking of the Sheet." It is found in several early books on music, i.e., Ballet's " Lute Book," and also " The Dancing Master, 1650-1."

So popular were these old dances of England that they were even introduced abroad. Horace Walpole, writing from Florence in 1740, says, " The Italians are fond to a degree of our country dances. ' Cold and Rain ' they only know by the tune. ' Blouzy-Bella ' is almost Italian. ' Buttered Pease ' is ' Pizzelli al buro.' "

How much more seemly, if not more graceful, this old-style country dancing than that in vogue in our modern ball-room, thronged with half-naked women clasped in the arms of some unknown man partner. It is no wonder that in some parts of rural France no dances but those by the lads and lassies in a " contre danse," i.e., one line opposite another, are sanctioned, or that till the Catholic Emancipation Act was passed in 1849 none of our old Catholic noblesse or gentry permitted their daughters to dance in any way except in the fashion of a " contre danse."

Let us be thankful that among the prevalent round dances of to-day one dear old country dance is preserved to us each Christmas in " Sir Roger de Coverley."

It would be wanting in this paper dealing with our
ancestors' Christmas if nothing was said about a very
important item with them in keeping Yuletide—
we mean their food and drink. What did our
forefathers eat? Or rather, what did they not eat?
So many things, and such astounding mixtures, that
one must think they had iron digestions.

Swans, bitterns, puffins, herons, cranes, curlews,
peacocks and porpoises, wine vinegar and verjuice in
one dish coloured with saffron and sweetened with
honey; salads of nearly all green herbs that grew; a
profusion of cinnamon, cloves, ginger, and no salt (in
cooking). Another peculiarity which shows itself in
everything they did—the garb they wore, the chairs
they sat on, the dishes they served—is the curious
distinction of rank: a whole animal, whether fish, fowl
or flesh, was only for a lord. When the master
of the house and his guests were commoners at the
Christmas table, everything down to a lark must
be "hewed on gobbets," i.e., cut into small pieces.
The mixtures, as we have said, in their dishes, were
wonderful. They mixed wine, milk and verjuice;
cheese, honey and raisins; rice, eggs, broth and
sweet wine.

Their principal wines were Gascon (Bordeaux)—
which country, long under our Angevin kings, ex-
ported much to this country—Malmsey (Malvoisie),
Romeney, and Osey. The last two were sweet wines.
Later, much sherry was imported, which, heated, went
under the name of "Sack." All these wines, as the
foods served up, were strongly spiced. Our forefathers

delighted in strong flavourings in all they drank and ate.

An Anglo-Norman carol gives us the names of where some of these wines came from:

" Seignors Noel beyt bien li vin Engleis
  E li Gascoin, e li Franceys
      E l'Angevin
  Noel fait beivere son veisin
  Si qu'il se dort, le chief enclin
      Sovent le jor
  Deu doint a tuz cels joie d'amours
  Qui à Dauz Noel ferunt honors.

  Seignors, jo vus di par Noel
  E par li sires de cest hostel
      Car bevez ben:
  Et jo primes beveren le men
  E pois après chescun le soen
      Par mon conseil
  Si jo vus di trestoy ' Wesseyl! '
  Dehaiz eit qui ne dirra ' Drincheyl! ' ' "

This old carol (of the early thirteenth century) is interesting in its final two lines, as incorporating in its Norman-French the Saxon drink-greeting of " Wassail and Drinkall." I give a translation of it:

" The English ale and Gascon wine
  And French doth Christmas much incline
      And Anjou's too.
  He makes his neighbours freely drink
  So that in sleep his head doth sink
      Often by day.
  May joy come from God above
  To all those who Christmas love.

Lords, by Christmas and the host
Of this mansion hear thee my toast—
   Drink it well—
Each must drain his cup of wine
And I the first will toss off mine:
   Thus I advise.
Here then I bid you all Wassail
Cursed be he who will not say Drinkhail
May joy come from God above
To all those who Christmas love."

At Christmas, particularly among the lower orders, heated beer was the great drink, and when it had apples floating in it, and by being thus heated had a white froth on its surface, it went under the name of "Lamb's Wool," or "Old Man's Beard." Home-made wine, distilled from cowslip, elder and currant, was industriously made against Christmas by the Ladye of the Manor in her "still-room," where she also compounded all the salves and lotions to dispense to her tenants and relations. The chemist and confectioner in the Middle Ages were the same person: then every lady who knew how to make pasties and such-like, knew how to make cordials and herb remedies.

We give here a carol sung by some of those Christmas guests who appear to have preferred old English beer to foreign wines:

"How butler, how! Bevis a towt (à tout)
Fill ye boll, jentill butler, and lett ye cup rowght![1]

---

[1] Go round.

Jentill butler, bellamy
Fyll ye boll by ye eye
That we may drynk by-and-bye—
With how, butler, how! Bevis a towt
Fill ye boll, butler, and lett ye cup rowght!

Here is mete for us all
Both for gret and for small
I trow we must the butler call—
With how, butler, how! Bevis a towt
Fill ye boll, butler, and lett ye cup rowght!

I am so dry, I can not speke:
I am ryght choked with my mete
I trow ye butler be a-slepe—
With how, butler, how! Bevis a towt
Fill ye boll, butler, and lett ye cup rowght!

If the butler's name be Water
I wold he were a galow-claper[1]
But if he bryng us drynk the rather
With how, butler, how! Bevis a towt
Fill ye boll, butler, and lett ye cup rowght! "

—From Hall's Collection.

Another carol of the time of Henry VI is still more imperative in language.   Evidently the man who composed it was a very thirsty soul, and meant to enjoy his Christmas in roaring way.   Here are four verses—it consists of eight.   The preface to it shows how the B.V.M. was appealed to in that age about matters we should now consider out of her province.

" Bring us in good ale, and bring us in good ale,
For our Blessed Lady's sake bring us in good ale.
Bring us in no brown bread, for that is made of bran,
Nor bring us in no white bread, for therein is no game:
But bring us in good ale!

---

[1] Gallows-bird.

Bring us in no beef, for there is many bones,
But bring us in good ale, for that goes down at once,
    And bring us in good ale!

Bring us in no bacon, for that is passing fat,
But bring us in good ale and give us enough of that!
    And bring us in good ale!

Bring us in no butter, for therein are many hairs,
Nor bring us in pig's flesh, for that will make us boars,
    But bring us in good ale! "

Perhaps of all carols dealing with the social side
of the Christmas rejoicings none is so well known, at
least by name, as " The Boar's Head Carol." This
was a favourite dish at this season with our forefathers; the forests then still which sheltered them
were numerous in England. It is not needful here
to go into the story of the Oxford Queen's College
student, whose exploits with a wild boar have
endured in " The Boar's Head Carol " and procession
annually at his college. Before his time such a dish
was well known, for among other instances we find
King Henry II, when his young son was crowned in
his (the father's) lifetime, serving at the coronation
feast at York a boar's head for his son's edification:
indeed, if we wish to trace the origin of serving up
the boar's head, we must go very far back.
Undoubtedly the custom takes its rise from an
ancient Babylonish " Sun Festival," during which a
wild boar was sacrificed to Adonis (or Tammuz), the
Sun God. Scandinavians, Egyptians, Indians,
Persians, Romans and others, alike at the winter

solstice held their Sun Festivals, at which an offering of a boar took place.

This carol is interesting in this: it shows from its alliterative use of Latin and the " mother tongue " how these two languages tried to gain the supremacy in the popular use.

" 1. The boar's head in hand bear I,
    Bedecked with bay and rosemary,
    And I pray you my masters be merry
        Qui estis in convivo
        Caput apri defero
        Reddens laudes Domino.

  2. The boar's head, as I understand,
    Is the rarest dish in all this land,
    Which thus bedecked with a gay garland
        Let us servire cantico
        Caput apri defero
        Reddens laudes Domino.

  3. Our steward hath provided this
    In honour of the King of bliss:
    Which on this day to be served is:
        In reginensi atrio
        Caput apri defero
        Reddens laudes Domino."

The third version from the Balliol MSS. has:

    " Caput apri refero
    Resonens laudes Domino."

It would be too lengthy to enumerate the many dishes, or all the recipes for making them, which graced a Christmas banquet.

Suffice it to mention some of the ingredients which

were not "home-grown." Plums were brought from
Syria by the Crusaders, and damsons from Damascus;
currants from Greece.　Jellies, gingerbread and
pickles are mentioned in the letter-book of Edward II.

Bread and butter dates from the reign of
Edward IV, before which dripping was used.
Chemists dealt in sweetmeats and spices, and women
were always the brewers.

About 1470, peers were allowed five dishes at a
meal besides pottage; gentlemen three; meaner
persons two.　Over-cooked meat was thought to
provoke bad temper. As to the ever-celebrated
"Christmas plum-pudding," it was made and eaten
in a liquid form.　It was a glorified "Furmety"—
still once a year eaten at St. John's College, Oxford,
when the Lesson of the day mentions Jacob's mess
of pottage.　Mince-pies in their present small form
seem of much later date.　The huge pies of currant,
fruit and other condiments were made, we know, but
these small pies seem forgotten.　It is probable the
cooks originally made them from the "leavings" of
the great pies that then graced every Christmas board.
At all events if, as sometimes now, they were called
by their varying shape, "High Church," or "Low
Church" mince-pies, they must date from the time
when the old Faith was prescribed in England.　It
has been affirmed their three ingredients—peel, meat
and currants—represent the gifts of the three Wise
Men, while if oval in shape they symbolized the Crib.
To show that there was plenty of material left after
making the huge Christmas pies to make these smaller

ones, we note even up to 1770 particulars of the immense pies. One such was shipped from Howick to Berwick to London for the use of Sir Henry Grey for his Christmas. It contained two bushels of flour, twenty pounds of butter, four geese, two turkeys, four wild duck, two woodcock, six snipe, four partridges, two neats' tongues, two curlews, seven blackbirds and six pigeon. It was made for him at Howick.

A later carol of the seventeenth century provides us with a sort of menu of one of these Christmas meals. It runs:

"My Lady Goose among the rest
    Upon the table takes her place,
  And piping hot bids do my best,
    And bravely looks me in the face:
For pigs and geese and gallant cheer,
    God bless my master and dame therefore!
I trust before the next New Year
    To eat my part of half a score.

I likewise see good mincèd pie,
    Here standing swaggering on the table!
The lofty walls so large and high
    I'll level down if I be able:
For they be furnished with good plums
    And spicèd well with pepper and salt,
Every prune as big as both my thumbs,
    To drive down bravely the juice of malt.

And then again my stomach I'll show,
    For good roast beef here stoutly stands,
I'll make it stoop before it goes
    Or I'll be no man of my hands."

It would ill become this essay if in conclusion we did not mention Christmas-boxes and Christmas gifts, which still obtain among us, but which date from a very early period.

The ancient Romans instituted under Servius Tullius the Paganalia, a holiday celebrated at the New Year. An altar was erected in every village, and there all persons gave money. Later, in Christian times, boxes were placed in the churches for receiving alms for the poor. Such boxes for Masses were also kept in the churches—sometimes for the sailors' safety on voyages, which on their safe return were opened. The boxes of this money were frequently opened at Christmas, hence Christmas-boxes.

Misson, the French traveller, mentions how gifts varied in time between his own country and England. He says, " Little presents are made from one another only on the first day of the year in France, they begin here at Christmas."

Queen Elizabeth relied on these gifts from her nobility, it is affirmed, to replenish her royal wardrobe. Peers and peeresses, bishops and clergy, servants of her household, even her master cook and sergeant of the pastry, were looked upon to give her valuable presents at Christmas. Sometimes in money: thus the Archbishop of Canterbury gave her one year £40; the Archbishop of York, £30. Among the gifts were rich petticoats, shifts, silk stockings (these were new to her, and she declared she never would wear in future anything else), precious stones, furs and bracelets. Her physician's gift one year was a box of green ginger; another, a box of foreign sweetmeats. Even her royal dustman's gift was a present of two bolts of cambric. Indeed, so onerous became these Christmas gifts to the Queen, and also to her successor, James I, that many of the nobility excused themselves by remaining in their own counties at Christmas, away from Court.

There are a great many more old customs than those briefly gone through in this essay, but space would not allow. Again, many of them obtained only in certain towns and villages, and were not therefore universal; but wherever they were, and whatever they consisted in, they showed how high was the estimation our ancestors regarded the Christmas festival and how each person contributed to its enjoyment.

This atmosphere now is greatly lost; the olden days have passed, and the pleasant, though perhaps false beliefs in the Christmas fairies, the Christmas omens and charms, the complete fraternization of poor and rich is broken and departed; we only have left to us a fragrant memory of this old social England of ours, and many of us think the world and our own Christmases the worse for that loss, still, though these social and pleasant facts have gone, the great spiritual fact remains till the end of time, that to us —as to our ancestors—" This day is born unto you a Saviour who is Christ the Lord."

And if shadowed by ugly rows of houses, distracted by motor traffic, offended by indifference and unbelief, we sigh for those far-off Christmases of old lang syne, have we not a force in memory that, as out of "the vasty deep," can bring them back to us, and, like a drift of white moonlight, fall on our sordid environments and lives, making the ugliest, for an hour, beautiful?

Referring to the carols given, and of course to very many more not given, it will be seen by the reader that after the Reformation period much of the mystic poetry is wanting in them. This is because the legends and cult of the B.V.M. and the saints, so conspicuous in the earliest carols, were debarred. The later ones, with a few exceptions, are in their subject convivial; the social side of Christmas takes the place of the spiritual.   Then again, the crisp, forcible way of composing in a few lines an episode which so eminently the old carols—like the old Border Ballads—possessed, is wanting in the later ones. As we began this essay by saying, carols to be as sweet as our forefathers heard or composed them, require the old environment.

ST. CLEER'S HOLY WELL, CORNWALL.

HOLY WELLS

WE can well understand, though we are not pagans, our remote ancestors looking on wells as holy places and under the influence of some being who there exercised beneficent influences. From remote ages flowing water and sparkling waves found in deep orifices had their fascination. This was intensified by the ancient belief that everything in the natural world was ruled by the supernatural. The storms that swept the lands and oceans, the trees that from time out of mind had stood unmoved beside their forest dwellings, braving the lightning or else struck as if a supernatural being was angry with it—the streaming meteors in the sky, oft-times the falling stars, the tremors of the earth when shaken by seismic influence, were all attributed not to natural but to supernatural influences. Why therefore, particularly as some of these wells, unknown to the dippers in them, or drinkers of them, really were chalybeate and possessed from natural causes healing powers—should they be excluded from the supernatural? And they were not; if we consider only the Roman period, the historian Diodorus (XI, 89) tells us in his day in the isle of Sicily were two prophetic wells called " Palice " (now rising into a small lake): these wells were agitated by volcanic springs. They were regarded especially under the care of nymphs or deities who watched over oaths. Therefore the most solemn oaths were

taken in their presence, and if those taking such oaths
perjured themselves they departed blinded.   And so
Seneca in his Epistle IV says: " We worship the head
of great rivers, and we raise altars to their first
springs. . . ."   Every river had its nymph presiding
over it.   Divination also was practised by the Latins
as by our early British and Celtic forefathers by
throwing a pin in the well, or needle, or coin, or other
small object, which, by judging the bubbles that arose
in the silent waters of the well or stream, would foretell
the fate of the thrower.   At Chester, for instance, a
large altar was found inscribed on two sides " Nymphis
et Fontibus," and close to the site of the well near by
large quantities of vases and coins and other little
objects thrown in, no doubt for talismanic and magical
purposes, or propitiations to the presiding spirit of
the well.

If this was all so to an educated and highly critical
race as the later Romans, it is little surprise that our
Celtic forefathers (for it was the Celts chiefly in this
country and their kindred in Brittany who most
cultivated the worship surrounding wells) have left us
so many wells under Christian names and a Christian
saint's invocation.   For when the Celtic population
became Christianized as well as their conquerors the
Saxons, the Church as she did in so often fixing a
pagan god's celebration, to one of her own, did the
same with the wells, for she remembered by His
Baptism, her Lord had hallowed the waters of Jordan,
and that He had not forbade the sick being healed by
being immersed when the angel ruffled the waters of

Siloam, so instead of heathen nymphs or a Celtic
and Druidic spirit presiding over the wells of Britain,
she blessed and consecrated them in a saint's name,
and endowed them with a saintly power.

If for no other reason in this matter-of-fact and
travelling age, it is kind of our remote forefathers to
have left us these "holy wells." Through the lovely
lanes and valleys of Cornwall, it gives an extra
pleasure to a ramble to come across these vestiges of
a long-past age. The sky seems bluer above them, the
bracken more golden around them, and even if we do
not believe now in their miraculous waters—to see
their tiny silver streams flowing from some hidden
water, or peer down into the depths of a fern-encrusted
well gives us something to remember for the good in
our wayside walks.

Again, for in this paper the writer, owing to want
of space, can only confine his more particular accounts
of these wells to Cornwall and Oxfordshire—to go
out of the ancient walls of that famed university town,
sitting in her wise state by the silver flowing Isis, and
discover as he turns over the musty records of the
past, that she too, this city of learning, had holy
wells, makes an additional charm, of an antiquarian
character, to his greater study of her ancient houses
of peace and learning.

So as we confine ourselves in this short essay to
the counties of Oxford and Cornwall, we will first
mention a few wells in and around Oxford.

Now I suppose everyone, from Don to under-
graduate, knows the name of St. Frideswide. If

K

nothing else would call her name to memory there is
the curious and ancient legend of her taking refuge in
a pigsty. As such with various episodes in her life
she is represented in the Cathedral Church of Christ-
church—a Princess who wished to vow herself to a
life of virginity, and beautiful exceedingly, she was
sought in marriage by a handsome prince, and fleeing
from his addresses after many adventures, escaped his
embraces. Now this saint, revered as she was and
her shrine intact in the Middle Ages, and to whom
much devotion was shown, seems not entirely to have
relied on her own powers of sanctity, for in the well
at Binsey, near Oxford, she called unto her help
St. Margaret. At the end of the chapel there is the
well still called after the latter saint. A certain old
English poet links these two saints together: " and a
cherche fayr and swete arerid (erected) in the honour
of her and St. Margrete," also " so sprong ther up a
welle, cler inowf and clene."

Over St. Margaret's well was a covering of stone,
and on it a picture of St. Frideswide or St. Margaret.
The well is about two miles from Oxford, and the
writer of the Denham tracts tells us " it was supposed
to have sprung from the prayers of St. Frideswide and
that many in olden times consulted it as an oracle on
the state of their burdened souls: maimed and sick
persons drank and bathed in its waters and were cured
by them. Now the stone edifice in the last century
destroyed has been restored." A descent of five steps
leads to an arch, beneath which is a basin containing
the holy water.

Another well, whose location now seems difficult to trace, was Showell or St. Bartholomew's well. The celebration of its existence was well known when Brand (Pop. Ant., II, 378) wrote. He says: " The fellows of New College in Oxford have time out of mind every Holy Thursday betwixt the houres of eight and nine, gone to ye Hospital called Bart'lemews neer Oxford, where they retire to ye chapell, and certaine prayers are read and an antheme sung: from thence they goe to the upper end of ye grove adjoyning to the Chapell (the way being beforehand strewed with flowers by the poor people of ye Hospitall); they placed themselves round about the Well there, where they warble forth melodiously a song of three or four or five parts: which being performed, they refresh themselves with a morning's draught there, and retire to Oxford before sermon."

Anthony Wood the antiquarian tells us of another well, evidently better known or more resorted to— for we find Oliver Sutton, Bishop of Lincoln, in 1291 sending to the archdeacon of Oxford a dire sentence of anathema and excommunication to those who should resort to it (the well of St. Edmund) for superstitious uses and pretending they found in its waters miracles like those contained in Holy Writ.

Anthony says: " But upon what account this well should be thus frequented, whether from the Saint's canonization in time of Henry II or upon any other event, I am in doubt. Yet for certaine if it was not for that particular it might arise from this, viz., that he, the said archbishop, while he was a student in Oxon

and counted by the greatest scholers of that age both
for his piety and learning, did often according to his
manner converse in privat with God, especially in his
walks of recreation in the fields neare Oxon " (St.
Edmund's Well was near the church of St. Clement,
outside Oxford), " of which Polycronicon also with a
specciall remarke tells us that he, one time as he
walked in a meede or feild neare Oxon, Jesus Christ
appeared to him and thence a well might reasonably
at that place burst forth even as St. Margaret's Well
at Binsey did at the intreatyes and converse with God
by St. Frideswyde."

This well was once famous for curing sicknesses
upon St. Edmund's Day. The day, something like
such days now abroad, was made a jovial holiday, the
people diverting themselves there with cakes, ale,
music and dancing. Another old writer tells us of
this well: " Near St. Clement's at Oxford was a spring
where St. Edmund, Archbishop of Canterbury, did
sometimes meet and converse with an angel."

Anthony Wood also mentions another well—now
quite forgotten. It lay at the east end of Crowell
Street, opposite the north-east corner of the ruins of
the city wall. It had a long history, for it was
mentioned in very ancient records, and in some as a
boundary to the lord (of the manor's?) rights between
it and the city liberties. In 1626 the Principal of
St. Edmund's Hall erected over it a stone pent-house,
and as the waters of this well had long been reported
to be good for bad sight, caused these two lines to
be carved on it with his arms:

> " There's none will hurt this well that's wise,
> For it hurts none but helps the eyes."

To which a waggish scholar wrote this answer with a piece of coal under it:

> " None but will hurt this well that's wise,
> For it helpeth none but hurts the eyes."

Another well must be mentioned, though now covered up or destroyed, because it gives its name to the well-known street in Oxford of Holywell. Very little, however, is known of its use and fame in the old days when wells were resorted to by the pious. Dr. Plot, in his " Natural History of Oxfordshire," says its waters were resorted to for bad eyes and other ailments. An old author makes mention of a holy man called Matthew that lived by the well, leading the life of a recluse or anchorite. That this well was of good repute in the Middle Ages we find from the fact that Fitzjames, the Warden of Merton, in 1488 built a fair house over it of stone. A token of his doing so long remained over the door leading to the well, of his arms carved, namely, " a dolphin naiant." Anthony Wood says of this well even in his time : " I find many persons relieved by those wholesome waters ; the water is very cold, but seldom freezes, and there is (for patients) a cold bath." This well was destroyed when the adjacent ground was drained to turn it into a cemetery.

These were the chief wells of Oxford. We would now ask the reader to follow us to the west country and trace some of the wells in Cornwall. Nearly all such are dedicated to saints little known—and few canonized, as it is called, at Rome. They were good men, sometimes chiefs of their communities, who came from Brittany or Ireland, or natives of Cornwall, to lead the ignorant inhabitants to a better Faith.

Near Liskeard, in a hilly and beautifully wooded country, is the well of St. Cleer. The baptistry or chapel by which the well was enclosed and an ancient cross about nine feet high form a group by the roadside a hundred yards eastward below the church. The chapel was destroyed by fanatics in the Civil Wars. It was restored in 1864. Its popularity in old times seems to have been from ducking mad people in the well as a cure. Yet the small space of the re-erected little chapel stands as an abiding witness to the reverence which in old times the Cornish people paid to springs of water—a feeling which is probably much older than Christianity, and one indeed which is in some degree common to the hearts of all men, as anyone may test who has ever on a burning day of midsummer come down, from the highlands, into a shady wood, weary and hot and thirsty. Then if he find by the wayside a cool crystal well, and drink from it, he will feel some emotion stirring in his heart which is not so very different from that which sanctified the wells long centuries ago.

Sometimes these wells beside the highway were used for a double purpose, being fitted with shelves in the sides above the water level, on which butter was set to cool. There is such a well in a lane at no great distance from that of St. Cleer.

Another well-known well is that of St. Keyne, near West Looe. It is covered by masonry, upon the top of which, formerly, grew five large trees. There now remain only two.

St. Keyne is said to have been an aunt of St. David of Wales. She had a nephew, St. Cradock. One day she met him and he stuck his staff in the ground which originated the spring, whereupon St. Keyne gave it to the people in return for the church which they had dedicated to her honour. Of old the waters were supposed to confer mastery in marriage to that one who drank them first. An amusing poem on this subject has been written by the poet Southey.

The Well of St. Keyne

" A well there is in the west country,
    And a clearer one never was seen,
There's not a wife in the west country
    But has heard of the well of St. Keyne.

An oak and an elm tree stand beside,
    And behind doth an ash tree grow,
And a willow from the bank above
    Droops to the water below.

A traveller came to the well of St. Keyne,
    Joyfully he drew nigh;
For from cock-crow he had been travelling,
    And there was not a cloud in the sky.

He drank of the water so cool and clear,
    For thirsty and hot was he,
And he sat down upon the bank
    Under the willow tree.

There came a man from the house hard by,
    At the well to fill his pail:
On the well-side he rested it,
    And he bade the stranger hail.

'Now art thou a bachelor, stranger?' quoth he,
    'For an', if thou hast a wife,
The happiest draught thou hast drank this day
    That ever thou didst in thy life.

Or hast thy good woman, if one thou hast,
    Ever here in Cornwall been?
For an' if she have, I'll venture my life,
    She has drunk of the well of St. Keyne.'

'I have left a good woman who never was here,'
    The stranger he made reply.
'But that my draught should be the better for that,
    I pray you answer me why.'

'St. Keyne,' quoth the Cornishman, 'many a time,
    Drank of this crystal well,
And before the Angels summoned her
    She laid on the water a spell.

If the husband of this gifted well
    Shall drink before his wife,
A happy man henceforth is he,
    For he shall be master for life.

But if the wife should drink it first,
    God help the husband then!'
The stranger stoop'd to the well of St. Keyne,
    And drank of the water again.

'You drank of the well I warrant betimes,'
    He to the Cornishman said:
But the Cornishman smiled as the stranger spake,
    And sheepishly shook his head,

' I hasten'd as soon as the wedding was done,
  And left my wife in the porch:
But I' faith she had been wiser than me,
  For she took a bottle to church.' "

St. Gulval's Well, in the parish of that name, was formerly in high repute. The people resorted there at feast time, and it was famous for its prophetic properties. An old woman stood by to whom the question of the future was propounded. For instance, if the question was about an absent friend, then if he was in health the water instantly bubbled; if sick, it became discoloured; but if dead it remained in its natural state.

Among some romantic scenery half hidden by trees, and about half a mile from St. Austell, is the enclosed little well known under the somewhat unpoetical name of Menacuddle (from the Cornish word for " hawkstone "). The chapel is eleven feet long and nine feet wide. The spring of water rises on the east side. It is also a wishing well. Surrounded with romantic scenery and covered with an ancient Gothic chapel overgrown with ivy, the virtue of its waters are far famed. Weak children have frequently been carried hither to be bathed in its silent stream. Ulcers have also been washed in its sacred water. A writer says within the memory of persons now living, this well has been a resort of the young for divination. On approaching its margin, each person, if he hoped for good luck through life, was expected to throw a crooked pin into the water, and it was presumed that the other pins which had been thrown there by former devotees might be seen rising from their beds to meet it before it reached the bottom.

St. Madron's Well has had many extraordinary properties ascribed to it. Here people subject to pains, aches, and stiffness of limbs congregated. Annual pilgrimage was made to it in ancient days. Only a century ago Borlase, the Cornish chronicler, said of this miraculous fountain: " The uneasy, the impatient, the fearful, the jealous, and the superstitious resort to learn their future destiny from the unconscious water. By dropping pins or pebbles into the water, by shaking the ground around the spring, by continuing to raise bubbles from the bottom on certain lucky days and when the moon is in a particular stage of increase or decrease, the secrets of the well are presumed to be extorted."

Of all writers, Bishop Hall of Exeter, in his book called " The Mystery of Godliness," when speaking of the good office God's angels do to His servants, says: " Of which kind was that noe less than miraculous cure which at Madern's Well in Cornwall was wrought on a poor cripple. I found neither art nor collusion the cure done there, the author an invisible God." This is very important evidence as coming from a Protestant bishop, and comparatively near our own times.

Like so many of these cures in this country and elsewhere, many must be attributed to the influence of the mind over the body, and though we are unprepared to say to a faithful heart and fervent faith, as the Almighty He permitted at the pool of Siloam cures, so such things are not impossible. We prefer ourselves in visiting these old wells to do so more as antiquarians and lovers of the past than as sick folk expecting miracles.

The hanging of rags or scraps of clothing on the branches of trees about Holy Wells has now died out —except, we believe, in Ireland. It was probably a remnant of old tree worship, and obtained all over the world. It was prohibited by the Church and mentioned as " vota arbores facere."

Far more lovely and beautiful now about these old wells of Cornwall, are the clustering ferns, in spring the purple violets and the pale primroses, while even the lichened stones give a beauty to the well, which when first built it never possessed.

To show how much the Medieval Church believed in the efficacy of wells when blessed by her, we give from the Roman Pontifical the form used for blessing such:

" We supplicants beg, O Lord, the mercy of Thy piety/grace that Thou wilt sanctify with Thy blessing the water of this holy well: and wilt grant to all the healthy enjoyment of life: and so Thou mayest suffer us to flee from every assault of the devil and temptation: that whosoever shall draw from this (well), whether to drink or for whatever necessities they shall employ its waters, they may severally/one and all enjoy the grace of virtue and of health: that so we may render thanks to Thee, O Lord, the sanctifier and saviour of us all. Through Christ our Lord."

NOTITIA HERALDICA

THE reigns of Edward III and Richard II were the palmy days of heraldry. The banners of war. refulgent with blazon, the lights of every chancel and hall stained with its tinctures, caused such an influence of heraldry upon the minds and passions of our rude forefathers which we cannot in these days realize, or how much it lent a powerful aid to the formation of our national character.

In its earliest formation coat armour was not necessarily hereditary. Many families retained no constant coat, but assumed now this, now that, sometimes their paternal, sometimes their maternal: again and perhaps it was owing to this arose the beautiful simplicity of those early coats, for the bearers of them chose such themselves, indeed some of the oldest coats have never been given or registered in the Heralds' College. The simplicity of these coats arose from the fact that those who designed them took the simple things around them to form the charges on them. (1) Thus the "chief" in this primitive heraldry was formed by turning back the upper part of a mantle, lined say with white, the mantle itself scarlet or blue. (2) A "bend"—a stripe passing diagonally across a shield—was copied from the leather belt worn over the shoulder of a knight. (3) A "fesse," too—a horizontal stripe across the middle of

156

COLLARS OF SAINTS.

(1) The upper one from the Effigy of Queen Joan at Canterbury, and

(2) The lower one from the Effigy of Robert, Lord Hungerford, at Salisbury

a shield—was taken from the military girdle or sash (derived from the French word *fascé*). (4) The " pale," in shape like the fesse, but its direction perpendicular, was derived from a palisade or piece of wood every soldier had to carry and fix in the ground for the security of a camp.   (5) The " scarbuncle " was copied from the cross-wise pieces of iron fastened behind a shield to strengthen it. (6) The " billets " were originally devised from the logs cut up for kindling the camp fires.   While (7) the " pile " was the sharp wedge used to fasten in the ground the ropes of the tents.   (8) The coat called " barry " of stripes was taken from the peace-robes of the knights, stripes being much in fashion ; so, too, when the coat was " bendy " it was copied from when these stripes ran perpendicularly.

Again, if we remember the dress of Richard II's time, we shall not be wrong in attributing the well-known blazon in heraldry of two colours on a shield called " counter-charged." In the illuminations of that period, the young knights appear in hose of two colours—white and red, blue and red, and so on. John of Gaunt appears in a long robe one half white, the other half blue, the colours of the House of Lancaster. The term " party per pale " no doubt arose from these variegated hose and clothes.

The colours, too, used in heraldry were also probably first taken from the garments of the early knights, who loved bright raiment. " Gules," the famous scarlet on many a shield, according to Ducange comes from the Latin word *guella*, i.e., the red colour of the mouth of an animal; or, according to others, from the Persian word *ghul*, signifying rose-red, the country of roses. Gules, therefore, was probably an imported colour by the Crusaders. It was sometimes called "vermeil" or "rouget," hence an old knight is said to have in the Roll of Caerlaverock—"mais eusmenions de la Butte La baniere eut toute rougeeté."

Azure also came from the East; it was a French corruption of the Arabic *lazur* or *lazuli*, the mineral of that colour. "Vert" is French, and was applied to everything that grew or bore a green leaf in the forest that might cover a stag, hence "vert" and "venison" were as inseparable as shadow and substance. This colour was frequently called "synople." So in the Book of St. Albans it appears "synobylt," from Synople, a town in the Levant where a green dye was procured.

As to "sable," the derivation is extremely obscure. It seems improbable it should have been derived from the little animal called "sable"—that animal was brown—and so many derive the word from "sabulum"—dark sand or gravel.

"Purpure" is little used in English heraldry. It is sometimes called "murrey," if so from the French word *morée* or the Italian *morella*—a dark cherry.

These early coats we have mentioned were sometimes blazoned not with the simple articles of everyday use the first bearers of them saw around them and depicted, but were allusive "charges" to the names of those that bore them, so called "armes parlantes."

Thus the Arundel shield, six swallows, from the French *hirondelles*; the Bacon shield—a boar; the ancient Rookwood one with chess rooks; the Pigots —pickaxes; the Wingfields—wings; the Boleyns— bulls' heads; the Shelleys—shells, and innumerable others.

Somewhat akin to these " armes parlantes " were the curious mottoes adopted by many families. " Honi soit," etc., of the Garter is well known, but another is more obscure of Edward III, i.e.:

> " Hay, Hay, the wythe swan,
>   By Gode's soul I am thy man."

Mottoes on ancient seals are extremely rare; from hundreds in the British Museum only about half a dozen have such. We here cite a few peculiar mottoes. That of the family of Dakyns of Derby- shire was, " Strike Dakyns, the Devil's in the Hempe." The Martin family of Dorset, whose crest was an ape, " He who looks at Martin's ape, Martin's ape shall look at him." The family of D'Oyley of Norfolk, " Do no yll quoth Doyle." That of Vere, Earl of Oxford, " Vero nil verius." That of Fitton, " Fight on quoth Fitton." That of Smith, " Smite quoth Smith."

Here we may mention that a great many of the arms of those classified as " armigere " were taken with small variations from their feudal lord's, whose influence extended over the lands they inhabited, just as in the same way in Scotland the dwellers on a feudal lord's or chief's estate took his name, and hence sprang many of the clans.

Quartering arms as times went by became very common, but in earlier times it was unknown. The first extant instance seems to have been that found on one of the so-called Eleanor Crosses (at Cheapside), where the arms of Edward I are quartered with Eleanor of Castile and Leon. None of the Barons' seals appended to Magna Charta show either quartering or impalement. Impalement seems to have arisen in the luxurious times of Richard II. After a time, so excessive did the practice of quartering become, that, as an instance, in the great hall of Fawnsley, Co. Northampton, the seat of the ancient family of Knightly, there is a shield containing three hundred and thirty-four quarterings. In mentioning quartering and impaling, the old herald, Nisbet, mentions a curious custom formerly in Spain, i.e., single ladies there divided their shields per pale, placing their paternal arms on the sinister side and leaving the dexter blank for those of future husbands. These, Nisbet says, were arms for young ladies resolved to marry, and were called "Arms of Expectation." Again, among the curiosities of early times may be mentioned "Adumbrated Charges," i.e., figures in outline, with the colour of the shield showing through, because the bearer of such retained only the shadow of their ancient dignities and former state. (Book of St. Albans.)

Kindred to badges was the rebus forming a pun on a man's name, and was at one time exceedingly popular. It no doubt originated in the canting or allusive heraldry of other days, like the boars' heads of the Swynfords, the trumpets of the Trumpingtons, the hammers (martels) of the Martels, or the scallop shells of the Scales.

A large number of rebuses on names ending in " ton " are based on a tun or barrel like the " lup " on a ton of Robert Lupton, provost of Eton (1503-4), or the large " kirk " and " ton " of Abbot Kirkton on the gate of the Deanery at Peterborough. Then there are the gold wells of Bishop Goldwell at Norwich; and the " eye " and the " slip " of a tree form, together with a man falling from a tree (I slip), the rebus of Abbot Islip at Westminster. An ox, the letter " N " and a bridge makes the rebus of Canon Oxenbridge in his chantry chapel at Windsor. Two large hares with a spring or well rising between them crouch at the feet of Bishop Harewell's effigy at Wells. A Sir John Pechey's arms in Lullingstone Church, Kent, are encircled by a wreath of peach blossoms bearing peaches. An author of to-day informs us a friend of his named Dorling has adopted as a rebus a little door (doorling). These rebuses were extremely common as used by merchants and others who had no claim to arms, and served to distinguish their goods and houses from others of a like class. They were, as we have seen from above, much used by ecclesiastical builders, who themselves, rising originally by their worth and learning from the lower classes, could not claim armorial bearings.

Badges of which the above were the offshoot were very extensively adopted and cherished in the Middle Ages. In some respects they were more popular than

L

the ancestral crest and coat of arms; probably because they were self-chosen in most cases, and did not, as their " coat " would, descend in fixed descent from an ancestor.   The most famous, of course, of these badges was that of the three ostrich feathers of the Prince of Wales, probably introduced by his mother, Philippa of Hainault, allusive of the County of Ostrevant—the appanage of the eldest sons of the House of Hainault.

The fetterlock and falcon and the white rose of the House of York, the white lion of the Earls of March, the rayed rose of Edward IV, and the silver boar of Richard III, are hardly worth mentioning, they are such familiar badges.   When badges first came into use is uncertain, but about the middle of the fourteenth century they abound.   They were embroidered on coverlets and hangings, while the emblazoned shield with the Knight's trusty sword hung up in the castle hall, ready for use on field and in tournament.   The embroidered badges were displayed in the ladye's bower and on her robes and beds.   Thus Edmund Mortimer left in 1380 a bequest of one large bed of black satin embroidered with white lions and gold roses.

In 1388 John of Gaunt willed his great bed of cloth of gold, powdered with roses of gold set upon pipes of gold and each pipe two white ostrich feathers.

Sometimes the badge was derived from part of the arms—such as the leopards' heads and wings of the de la Poles, and the water-bourgets of the Bourchiers, or the silver star of the Veres.   As a writer says:

" If by chance a badge could have any punning or allusive meaning, it was more popular, and it then often saved making a rebus." Thus the boar (verre) of the Veres; the crab or the scrap of the Scropes; the pike or the luce of the Lucys; the longsword of Longespee; the "gray" or the badger of Richard, Lord Grey of Codnor; and the woodstock or tree stump of Thomas, Duke of Gloucester, who was born at Woodstock, are examples of badges of this character. Sometimes, as in the case of Lord Grey of Codnor, and Stanley, Earl of Derby, both arms and badge occur on their seals. Sometimes, too, the badge was a knot—such as the celebrated House of Audley used, and also the Bourchiers and the Staffords and other noble families.

Somewhat kindred to badges are the distinctive livery collars which were worn in the Middle Ages by people of rank. Beads and some adornment of the neck seem to have had an allurement for all ages and all people, from the savage of the Dark Continent to the refined and polished nations of antiquity. It is therefore no surprise that in the Middle Ages, when both men and women delighted in bright colours and ornaments, collars of a distinctive character were much in vogue. We are not here referring to the collars of Knighthood, such as in this country the Garter, or the Bath, or the numerous ones of a military character in that home of Knighthood— France. These collars were of a non-military type, often conferred, like livery, by some powerful noble on his followers and relations. They were sometimes made of velvet or other stuff, with ornaments sewn on them; others had links joined together composed of silver gilt or other metal.

The most known, and whose meaning and origin is most debated, is the collar of SS. In their perplexity for its meaning some writers have given it even an oriental origin. It is generally credited to have been the distinctive badge of the House of Lancaster, and given to supporters of the Red Rose; on the other hand we find Yorkists possessing it. Thus, in one of the windows of the chapter house at Wells is a shield of the arms of Mortimer and next to it a gold star within the horns of a crescent party blue and silver encircled by a collar of SS also half blue and white. Again, on the south side of the choir of Ely Cathedral is the effigy of John Tiptoft, Earl of Westmorland. About his neck appears the collar of SS, though he was an ardent and distinguished Yorkist, and was executed by the Lancastrians in 1470. This collar of SS seems to have been in most cases sewn or worked upon a band of silk, velvet or other material, or, as has been said above, of linked metal. It was worn by persons of every description, from the King and Queen to the Knight and Squire; it was also worn by their wives.

A difficulty has always arisen as to the meaning of those two letters of SS. Did they stand for " souvenance " (remembrance) or " souvereyn " (sovereignty)? If the first, was it a gentle reminder, invented by Henry of Lancaster, to his party while he was in exile of his claims to their fidelity? It certainly seems—though we have the difficulty to surmount of certain Yorkists wearing it—to have been invented by Henry (afterwards the fourth of that name) before his accession.

That it had some Lancastrian significance seems borne out by the fact that on the triumph of the White Rose, Edward IV invented a rival collar composed of blazing suns and York roses disposed alternately. Thus on the Neville tomb at Brancepeth, the Earl's countess has on a collar of alternate suns and roses. After the accession of Henry VII, this collar was in some cases altered. Thus the effigy at Salisbury of Sir John Cheyney, K.G., 1489, has appended to his collar of SS a large portcullis charged with a rose. Also a brass at Little Bentley, Essex, has the collar on its effigy of SS with a portcullis pendant.

One of the strangest collars extant on an effigy is found at Ripon, of Sir Thomas Markenfield, who displays a collar formed of park palings which widen out in front to enclose a couchant hart. (W. H. St. John Hope.)

At Wooton-under-Edge the brass of Lord Thomas Berkeley has a collar sown with mermaids, the cognizance of his house.

The sole remainders of these civilian, in opposition to military collars, are to-day to be found in the civic chains of mayors and such officials, which have become elongated into chains. Perhaps the nearest approach to these ancient and in many cases beautiful collars of the medieval period, is the broad band called a " dog collar " of some fayre

ladye going to Court, composed of rare pearls ٹr
diamonds.

When we study old wills and inventories few can
have failed to notice what a large part was played by
heraldry in the household effects of our ancestors.
The vestments of the chapels and chantries embroidered with such, the hangings that covered the rough
surfaces of the great hall, the hangings and curtains
of the beds, the plate on the great sideboards, the
beakers—all had heraldic mottoes, badges, and, in
the merchants' houses, frequently punning rebuses on
them. We need hardly mention the monuments and
stained glass blazoned with heraldic shields, for it is
from them we are chiefly able to trace the connection
of long dead families with their present-day repre-
sentatives. For this reason they are most valuable.

Since heraldry is a survival of what was once a
living thing, it cannot be too much impressed on the
modern delineator of such that birds and other
animals should be blazoned in a conventional manner.
Wyverns, two-headed eagles, griffins, never, for
instance, existed except in the pages of the Bestiaries.
Even lions, the heralds—unless travellers from afar
—never saw; their ideas of such were always imagin-
ative, and—as they followed each other's steps—
conventional. In this fact really exists their beauty
on ancient shields, for who can compare, for instance,
the elegance of the long-clawed lions on the tombs
of our early kings at Westminster with the fat, well-
fed lions in the pages of our modern peerages?

Again, the modern delineator forgets the greater

beauty of the old herald in blazoning charges. The modern one places his charges in small dimensions on his shield, while the older one fills up the whole surface, as far as possible, with, for instance, his rampant lion, or his impossible griffin.

The old days have passed away when heraldry, not only on the field of battle and tournament, helped to distinguish one knight from another, but also those days when, carved on the tomb of the dead, emblazoned on the manor and castle walls, or figured on the rich robes of the gentry and nobility, it brought to their minds the elevated thoughts of those who first bore its bright colours in many a brave action, perhaps at Senlac, or Poitiers, or Agincourt, when heraldry, therefore, like a brave admonition, had a vital and useful purpose. To-day its voice becomes weaker and weaker, and perhaps its only use nowadays is to help trace by its shields in some church window or on the silent effigies of some of those who lived in " old times gone," the lineage of their descendants.

MISERICORDS

THE pilgrim to our ancient cathedrals or churches can realize their interesting remains in two ways: (1) he can take a broad cursory view of them, and by that broad view he can fill his artistic soul with a general sense of beauty; or (2) he can spend hours upon hours in an intensive view of the same, whereby he will discover many hidden beauties, curious emblems and strange carvings, done when all the world was younger and simpler than now. The broad cursory view lifts a man's soul, perhaps, best nearer the eternal; for instance, few who have stood within the west door of Winchester Cathedral and seen pillar upon pillar, and arch upon arch springing upwards, as it were from earth to heaven, has not received a better medicine for his soul than from all the drugs of the alchemist.

So likewise the traveller over seas, who has stood in the noble cathedral of Chartres and caught the magic radiance of its wonderful glass, embroidering the cold stones as with jewelled fingers of light, has he not gained much in his perception of the beautiful?

It is by this comprehensive and all-embracing view of these splendid survivals of the past, that we best realize the whole plans which were in the artist's mind ere the first block of stone was cut, or the first saint in his glory set up in his noble window.

168

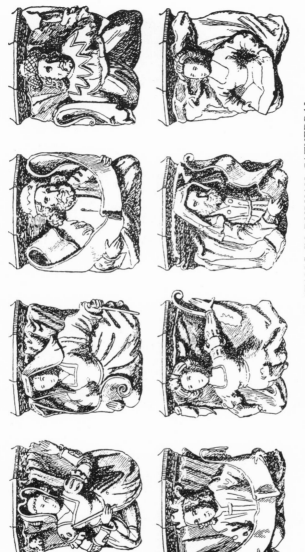

CARVED FIGURES ON THE STALLS IN DURHAM CATHEDRAL.

Yet the other and more minute examination (one which certainly cannot be undertaken by the wayfarer who spends a brief half-hour, led on by an impatient verger) will well repay a deeper, and perhaps a more interesting study. We must ever remember in this hurried age in which we live, and in which all our buildings are erected by contract, that the procedure in building in the Middle Ages was on a far different principle, and with a different result. There was no scamping in that work; whether it was to be detected or not, whether one part remained in the shadows or could be seen in the broad light of day, the work was as perfect. The tiny chantry of some benefactor had the same minute attention bestowed on it as the great pulpit in the nave. Is it any wonder therefore that the carvings on the stalls or the half-seen misericord seats, to those who have leisure to examine them, have a great artistic worth? The misericords are especially rich in carvings of the quaintest description.

They were originally devised for those wearied by standing during the long offices of the Church. These seats are known by a variety of names—misericords, misereres, subsellæ, sellettes, and sometimes (in a tell-tale fashion) " nodding seats," from the popular notion that if the occupant, during a long service, was inclined to sleep and bend forward, they would fall down with a crash.

Now some of the frequent carvings on these seats are extremely strange; some are attacks on the monks, some scenes with animals, some with secular persons employed in secular service. It has been supposed by some that many of the carvings were intended by the monks as a satire on the secular clergy, or on rival monastic bodies, particularly on the mendicant friars. Others have contrived to see a deep symbolic meaning in every group. When we examine the carvings of some—those of animals—it certainly seems to show great largeness of mind in the Medieval Church.

That miracle plays took their origin in the church buildings and by the ecclesiastics acting even as buffoons, we know; that, too, the church was often the meeting-place of guilds and secular bodies, and was used for many other civil purposes that they are not now used for. As one learned writer has suggested, when pictures were few, and the power to read rare, these misericord carvings were the " genre " pictures and story-books of the Middle Ages. Again, it has been suggested for some of the strange subjects of the carvings (as the stalls the misericords were attached to were generally appropriated to a particular benefice or prebend) that the carvings might have some satirical allusion to the stall-holder's character, or the parish he represented. Others, and certainly with some foundation, knowing how certain vices and virtues were symbolized by animals, have felt their existence to be in that fact.

The period in which carved misericords were made in this country extends through several centuries. The earliest known series is at Exeter and dates from the thirteenth century. During the fourteenth and fifteenth centuries the workmanship on these little

seats was at its best. Many have perished along
with the beautiful Abbeys containing them; many,
especially in village churches, by the hands of
ignorance and bigotry.

Perhaps the chief home of these little carved seats
is in Norfolk. There, not only the chief ecclesiastical
buildings and lesser churches possess a great many of
them, but they are peculiarly quaint and realistic.
These carvings were chiefly the work of Flemish
artists, who came over in the reign of Edward III and
settled in the eastern counties. Bands of workmen
went from place to place, and were often attached to
a church. These were specially versed in ecclesiastical
legend, and the traditions of their times.

A great work, used for these carvings of grotesque
animals, was the well-known " Bestiaria," or Books of
Beasts, that is of living creatures in general, where
each animal was so treated that his or her peculiarities
should convey a wholesome moral.

In the Middle Ages these books were very popular
and furnished materials for many sermons, particularly
those of the Friars, who went from village to village
preaching, wherever they could obtain an audience for
their simple eloquence and quaint appeals. Thus
their sermons, introducing animals that could be both
good and bad, were fellows to the old Mystery and
Morality Plays, both being a strange medley of moral
teaching and broad humour. Again, if these animals
appear to us so distorted from nature, we must
remember how little facilities our ancestors possessed
for seeing the originals. Travellers to strange

countries were many, but few, if any, could draw the likenesses of the strange beasts they met with, and it was their tongues that alone described them.

The first English menagerie was at Woodstock in the time of Henry I, and was transferred to the Tower of London in the reign of Henry III.

Perhaps the most powerful of the Fables that influenced the carvers of misericords in this country and in France, was that of " Reynard the Fox," begun in the twelfth century, a long satirical poem by Reineke Fuchs. Up to the fifteenth century it became universally popular. Reynard represents the Church continually warring with his uncle Isengrin the Wolf, who stands for the feudal baron. Nodel, the lion, less carnivorous, represents Royalty.

On the Bristol misericords no less than nine subjects appear to have been taken from this work.

In these quaint carvings we find (1) the wildness of imagination and roughness peculiar to the northern nations; (2) the great variety of them, so few are alike; (3) the naturalness of the beasts and birds attempted to be depicted, that is, as far as the artisan's knowledge went, derived, as has been seen, from the books of Bestiaria, or the description of travellers, or the outcome of legend. Differing from the formality of the ancient Greek artist, handed down to the Byzantine, the Gothic artist tried to break away from a set formalism in his work. (4) The medieval artists were seldom grave and solemn; they had with their age—even in dealing with sacred things—a touch of humour, which led them, when carving these misericords and bosses and corbels in the churches, to love to produce the grotesque; it was an age of jest, and in their work with their chisels they jested. In this way these strange little carvings became illustrated chronicles of the ages their makers produced them in, and so are exceedingly interesting and useful. As a learned writer has pointed out, " they —these early artists—used their chisels, not to record, but in a gay way to warn, to encourage, to guide, to beautify and to criticize."

Thus they were influenced, it is true, by the traditions of their art, but they never let that tradition trammel their feelings or their own experience, or the customs and legends of the less educated for whom they built their churches or carved their grotesque fables and animals.

It is impossible in an essay to describe the endless varieties of these carvings. A certain number, as examples, we here submit:

Exeter Cathedral has a very fine collection of misericords that date from the middle of the thirteenth century. Among them (1) a figure of a man's head crowned with four legs, hands in front, hoofs behind. The body has a cloth over it and a saddle, with stirrups, supposed to represent Nebuchadnezzar in his debasement. (2) A knight in a boat, towed by a fine swan. The knight is in chain armour, with surcoat, and a late form of bascinet helmet.

In some misericords owls are represented. In a Latin poem occurs the line "Christus a noctuis datar supplicis " (Christ was put to death by owls), for in the celebrated Bestiary Jews are compared to the night raven or owl, which cannot endure the sun, more than the Jews the Son of Righteousness.

On the stalls of the choir in Boston Church are carvings of pigs playing on the organ or harp.

A writer on poppy-heads says: " Some of the grotesque carvings teach a wholesome lesson. One of this character in the choir of Chester Cathedral represents a beast with the face of a voluptuous drunkard, lifting a tankard to his lips, whilst the devil kneels below, forcing the tankard upwards to the toper's mouth."

Mr. Collins tells us: " Frequently the fox is represented as preaching in a monk's or friar's habit to geese and other creatures, as on the stalls of Beverley Minster, St. Mary's, Beverley and Ely Cathedral." And again, " At Worcester Cathedral there are carved on a misericord foxes running in and out of holes. St. John the Evangelist stands near by with his Gospel in his hand and his eagle at his feet. Here we see an allusion to our Saviour's words ' Foxes have holes,' etc., in St. Matthew viii. 20. It has been supposed that the object of this particular carving is to induce him who sees it to choose between good and evil."

At Winchester Cathedral a misericord has two dogs standing on their hind legs, their muzzles together; a boar playing the viol while another listens, and a sow playing a double pipe while supplying her litter with requisite nourishment; a little pig listens enchanted in the background.

Two of the misericords from St. Katherine's by the Tower (now in the chapel in Regent's Park) have: (1) a lion devouring a dragon, and two dragons curled round like serpents; (2) an elephant with a castle on its back from which rises a crowned female head.

In " The Romance of Symbolism " Mr. Sidney Heath tells us that the phœnix was derived from the Egyptian Bennu, a sort of heron, the emblem of the rising of the sun, the return of Osiris to the light, and that the story of it springing from the ashes is of much later date. Also that Lactantius (A.D. 300) wrote a poem on the bird in which he tells us : " Happy is it to need no marriage." Rufinius, a hundred years later, used this story as an argument in support of the Incarnation. " Why should it seem wonderful that a Virgin should conceive when the eastern bird appears to be born or re-born without a consort? for he is always only one, and ever succeeds himself by birth or re-birth." In the Catacombs the phœnix is nimbed and perched on the boughs of a tree beside St. Paul, and on the ancient basilica of St. Paul at Rome a sculptured figure of the phœnix, together with its name, appears over the doorway.

The ape has been used to represent Satan, denoting hatred, malice and hypocrisy. The swan is the emblem of solitude. The cock is not always associated with St. Peter, but also typifies the Resurrection, our Lord having broken out of the grave at cock-crow.

A misericord at Great Malvern Priory depicts three rats hanging a cat by a rope pulled over a crossbar. The rats are hauling at the rope, the cat looking quite unconcerned.

St. George's Chapel, Windsor, has a dog taking meat out of a pot on the fire, while three other dogs try to get it, one of them gripping a hind leg of the successful dog in its jaws. A cook with a knife is looking on.

In the sister chapel, known as " Henry VII's," at Westminster Abbey there is a group of apes; one has fruit in his hands, the other a young one on her knee and another by her side. To the right is a monkey chained to a block, holding up a bottle; to the left a bear, with collar and chain playing bagpipes.

Before concluding this article on the subject of beasts and other grotesque creatures in the misericords, and other carved material in our old churches and cathedrals, besides the theories before stated for their presence, may be added another, i.e., that from the earliest ages the fabric of the church was used to represent the ark (ship) in which all created flesh was saved. Hence the admission of these creatures of the lower creation was allowed in the Christian ark, to exemplify that within it, as of old, all created beings were saved. At all events the theory is worth considering, and as the choir sang the song of the three children, "All ye works of the Lord bless ye the Lord," from under the seats of the stalls, or from the lofty bosses, a voice might seem to echo even from these lesser creatures: " We too praise the Lord."

THE GLASTONBURY TRADITION

A TRADITION should possess three elements for its acceptance or belief:

(1) It should have an element of reasonable probability.

(2) It should not run counter to any known historical fact.

(3) It should fulfil the law laid down by Vincent de Lerins in matters of the Faith, have been received by all men in all places and at all times.

In this paper it is therefore proposed to test the tradition that Joseph of Arimathea came to Britain and first preached to its indigenous population Christianity, by seeing if these three elements can be found in that tradition.

Taking the first, i.e., that the tradition should possess a reasonable element of probability. Such is found to be the case. From the little we find recorded of Joseph in the Gospels we gather he was a man animated with one of the elements every missionary must have—never to be ashamed of his faith; that despite, too, being a rich man, he never put the fear of imperilling his wealth before that of his faith; that he possessed the great virtue of missionary life—he conceived his plans boldly, and boldly brought those

177   M

plans to success. To amplify this a little more, he
was bold in profession of his faith, for when other
disciples at the Crucifixion fled, he arose serene and
stately in the integrity of faith, and by begging the
Body of the dead Christ, declared himself a follower
of the Crucified. Again, being rich did not hamper
him in doing this, even if in that corrupt age it might
bring upon that wealth confiscation, or upon himself
imprisonment (which, according to tradition, it did).
Lastly, he conceived—no doubt when standing viewing
afar off the Crucifixion—his determination to bury
in his own sepulchre this dying Christ, and that
conception was wrought out when, notwithstanding the
jeers of the rich Jews, his relatives, he anointed this
Body with spices and buried It in his garden-tomb.
These incidents all prove that Joseph possessed the
essentials necessary for a preacher and a missionary.

Again, and here we have to fall back on the legend
itself to prove its probability: On the night after
placing in the tomb our Lord, the Jews, for such an
open defiance, imprisoned him, and after forty days
in that confinement—according to one account, himself,
in another, an angel—opened his prison doors and set
him free. Now this is certainly highly probable, if
we believe the accounts in the Acts that Peter was
delivered from his bonds in a like manner. Why
should the devout man, Joseph, who had anointed his
Master, less than Peter who had denied him, be
delivered from prison? The tradition has an element
of reasonable probability.

Again, set free he wends his way to his home,

Arimathea. Here the Jews follow him and to get rid of such an inconvenient believer in the Crucified—a man, too, having a high position in the country—place him adrift in a small boat with Mary Magdalene and her sister Martha and Lazarus, persons also awkward for the Jews as followers of the same Christ, and witnesses of one of His greatest miracles. The tradition says, tossed about for some days they drifted along the Mediterranean till cast ashore in Provence.

We are not here to try and prove if this story of Mary and Martha and Lazarus may be highly probable or not, but our eyes are fixed on that small vessel in which Joseph is said to have been cast adrift, and we say it has a high probability that, seeing they found imprisonment useless, to get rid of him altogether by possible shipwreck was to them a clever thought. That shipwrecks often took place in that Middle Sea we know. Paul himself could witness to that at a later date. A light boat would be carried, too, a long way—it is not the least out of the range of possibility it drifted till it reached the shores of Provence.

In the legend of the Holy Grail it is mentioned that Joseph brought with him his wife and children. We are of opinion this is only an insertion, and more probably he was unmarried, and it was only inserted in order to be able to prove King Arthur was his descendant, and so connect Glastonbury, whither Joseph went with Arthur in the quest of the Holy Grail by his knights. Be that as it may be, it seems very unlikely, if it is true, that when he was cast adrift in a small boat by the Jews, they should have been so nicely careful of his feelings as to have included his wife and children, particularly if they did, as the tradition says, also in the same boat, ship with him Mary, Martha, and Lazarus. In the tradition proper of Joseph there is, when mentioning his arrival at Glastonbury, no mention of such wife or sons.

At what date Joseph landed on the shores of Provence it is difficult to say. If, as I have stated above, he proceeded after forty days' imprisonment, begun on the evening of the day of Crucifixion, to Arimathea, where he stayed surrounded by his enemies, it seems most probable they shipped him adrift in this open boat very immediately. If this were so, then allowing for a month in his own country and a possible twelve days in the open boat on the Mediterranean, this would make his landing in Provence A.D. 33. On the other hand, two medieval Lives of Joseph state he remained in Palestine till the death of the Blessed Virgin, thus in the medieval " Lyfe of Joseph of Arimathea," by Richard Pynson, 1520, he says :

> " Now here how Joseph came into Englande
> But at that tyme it was called Brytayne
> Than XV yere with our lady, as I understande
> Joseph wayted still to serue hyr he was fayne."

Now if he waited thus for her death, which is generally supposed to have been about thirty years after her Son, it would bring the date of Joseph's landing in Provence to about A.D. 63-64. Of course,

knowing the prevalent disposition at the time this
" Lyfe " was composed, of introducing the Blessed
Virgin into all the legends and pious romances as
possible, one must not altogether trust this assertion
that Joseph waited in Syria till the death of the
Virgin. On the other hand, if we can get over that
rather difficult fact that for nearly thirty years Joseph
was no more molested in his native place, it allows
him to grow old—which, certainly by the tradition, he
was when he arrived in Britain. Say he was, as
probably having entered into his patrimony at the
time of the Crucifixion, thirty to forty years of age, if
he waited another thirty for the Virgin's death this
would make him, allowing some little while in
Provence and Gaul, about sixty-four years of age.

This later date of his arrival there seems best to
fit in with the statement that he found St. Philip in
Gaul preaching the Gospel. The Apostles, we know,
travelled into many countries, but if the tradition is
true that in Upper Asia Philip first began his labours,
it would, this later date of him being in Gaul at the
time of Joseph's arrival there, better synchronize with
the tradition, for it is a far cry from Upper Asia to
Gaul, especially remembering the difficulties in those
days of travelling.

Arrived in Gaul, meeting the Apostle, seeing with
his own ardent missionary spirit, which has before
been touched on, the many converts St. Philip was
making, it is a great probability of the truth of the
tradition that Joseph sought some place where he, too,
might bring heathen into the fold, nor is it improbable

that the great island of Britain daily and dimly seen by him, if living by the coast of Gaul, should have been the spot he chose.

Long before there had been great communication between that island and Gaul, particularly that portion of the latter called Brittany. There a similar Celtic population and speech was found, and there, according to an ancient writer cited by Michelet the islanders were used to carry over in their frail boats at dead of night their dead for burial. So we still see in Brittany an immense number of Druidical stones for such rites of sepulchre and propitiation to the solar deity.

The question now arises why Glastonbury, then called Ynswytryn, was the object of Joseph's journey when he came to Britain. In the memorials of the Apostle's work they always, in missionary zeal, seemed to have penetrated into the very strongholds of false religions—thus Paul at Ephesus, Peter and Paul at Rome. Glastonbury had long been one of the sacred places of Druidic worship. A present-day writer asks: " Is it too much of a conjecture that the Christian Church may have taken the place of some Celtic Temple or holy spot especially devoted to the cult of the dead and of that of the Lord of the Shades from which the Celts feigned their descent? " It certainly is no conjecture, this place afterwards called Glastonbury stood on ground surrounded by water and was called by the Britons " Ynswytryn," or the Glassy Island, from the colour of the stream which circled it. Afterwards it obtained the name of

Avallon, either from Aval, an apple which abounded there, or from a British Chief named Avallon.

For Druidic worship it was particularly fitted. Running water symbolized fertility; fertility depended on the solar deity. The Druids were certainly sun worshippers. It is no wonder, therefore, that on the site of running water, Glastonbury, with also its nearness comparatively to the sea, where was situated the Islands of Happiness, for the Celtic dead had rude temples and cromlechs before it became the centre of Christianity for western Britain. The very name of Avallon even now is enchanting.

> " Where falls not hail, or rain, or any snow,
> Nor ever wind blows loudly; but it lies
> Deep meadow'd, happy, fair with orchard lawns
> And bowery hollows crowned with summer sea."

Here should the old Celtic myths and worship give place to that of the Crucified, and here for long time afford a place for the new religion to the wild tribes around.

So Joseph decided therefore on Ynswytryn as his goal.

It will be seen from the above account of this tradition so far as the material in hand of Joseph's life in Palestine, and his missionary spirit, his courage, his perseverance, and his exposure in a boat which drifted him to Provence where he met Philip and crossed ultimately, and his proceeding, to Glastonbury, there is nothing in the tradition which is not extremely probable, with the exception of his being freed from prison by Christ or an angel, the supernatural which so often causes doubt to arise as to the veracity of a legend—when it is found there—is entirely absent.

If all this had been recorded in one of the canonical books—say the Acts of the Apostles—it would appear no more out of the ordinary in the recital of early apostolic labour than that of St. Paul. It possesses more circumstantial detail than several of the received accounts of the labours in foreign lands of some other well-known Apostles of the Faith. All this shows the tradition has a very great possibility.

(2) We will now touch on the second proposition we laid down when we began to treat of this subject, i.e., that a tradition should not contravene any known historical fact.

It is quite assented to by all historians that long before the coming of St. Augustine there had been a Christian Church founded among the Britons. Who founded it? For such things do not spring up in a night, a day, or a year; wherever such has been founded in the centre of an alien faith and religion means many labours, much wisdom, and perseverance.

There are two accounts of how and by whom Christianity was introduced here.

We will take the one first which on the face of it seems adverse to our contention in favour of Joseph having been the first who brought the Faith here.

Bede, " Eccles. Hist.," i, 4, writes : " In the year 156 from our Lord's Incarnation, whilst Elentherius, a holy man, was vested with the pontificate of the Roman Church, Lucius, King of Britain, sent him a letter praying to be made a Christian by an act of his authority—the object of which pious request he soon after obtained, and the Britons having received the faith from Lucius, kept it whole and undefiled and in peace and quiet till the days of the Emperor Diocletian."

The other is about sixty-three years after the Incarnation of our Lord. St. Joseph of Arimathea, accompanied by eleven other disciples of St. Philip, was despatched by that Apostle into Britain to introduce in the place of barbarous and bloody rites, long exercised by the bigoted and besotted Druids, the meek and gentle system of Christianity (excerpt from Dugdale's " Monasticon ").

(*a*) Now we would observe both these accounts are on one plane—they are traditional. Unless Bede had some MSS. of which we do not know, his knowledge of Lucius as the mainspring for the first introduction of Christianity, to the British nation, rests on no more firm historical ground than the other tradition that Joseph of Arimathea was that introducer.

(*b*) We know nothing of this King Lucius, except by tradition. His name—unless rendered afterwards into Latin, and then it was no Celtic name under a Latin disguise—is certainly not British. Even unlike that rather mythical prince—Arthur—he just appears in this place and then sinks into obscurity. Gildar, who is answerable for his appearance in history, gives no distinct information. He may have been a king, but certainly only one of those petty kings who in British, as after in Saxon, England, had one of the many kingdoms or chieftainships in the land.   On the other hand, the other competitor (Joseph) introducing Christianity here we know from the orthodox Gospels something about, both in his character and in his position, and that he existed.

Is it not possible that these two accounts can be harmonized, and that without disproving the accuracy of either?   We know in later Saxon times, and even after the coming of St. Augustine, one Saxon kingdom was still pagan, while another would have accepted Christianity.   Is it not quite feasible that the part of Britain, when Lucius (if he did) sent to Rome to have it Christianized, was then pagan, while in the west country, of which Glastonbury was the centre, Christianity had, from Joseph in the year A.D. 63, prevailed?   Knowledge in those days, with unpassable forests, no roads, and wild tribes, intervening, and constant internecine feuds, kept large communities—who in those days would share a common religion—far apart.

Again, we know how quickly the flame of first religious ardour dies out.   In the after Saxon little kingdoms one would be for a time Christian, then fall back into the old gods' laps; when Lucius wrote, as it is said, to Rome for an instructor in Christianity, that Christianity introduced much earlier by Joseph might have died out, and so indeed we are told " that this holy place which had been the abode of saints became after the decease of St. Joseph and his companions, a den of wild beasts till Lucius's days " (Cressy's

" Eccles. Hist.," ch. 7); " yet 'tis certain they left behind them some disciples either on the island (Avalon) or in its neighbourhood, or else how could Eluanus and Medioinus have been instructed in Christianity. Now all historians agree these two messengers of King Lucius sent by him to Rome were already Christians " (Cressy).

In comparing these two accounts of those who first introduced Christianity—though we have shown they might, though divergent, yet be harmonized—it is well to point out that of the two traditions that of St. Joseph is much the older. His advent to Britain is placed A.D. 63-64. Now Bede, who wrote his history, which is the chief source for the other tradition of King Lucius, died in the year A.D. 785, more than seven hundred years after St. Joseph arrived in Britain, and from which date this tradition of his coming has continually been preserved. Again, let us ask those who endeavour to ridicule this tradition of Joseph of Arimathea finding a resting at Glastonbury, by saying it was originally invented by the early Christian Britons to show their Church had a founder who had met and seen their Lord, why did they not—unless they knew that Joseph had introduced to their fathers Christianity—choose an Apostle as their founder? If a legend was about to be fabricated it was as easy to make Peter or Paul, or James or Philip, to have come to the shores of Britain, as it was to invent Joseph of Arimathea, who was not one of the apostolic hierarchy, who had written no Gospel and no epistles. The

answer to all this evidently is, Joseph was chosen
because the tradition of him being the introducer of
Christianity to Britain our forefathers knew was a true
one.

(3) We now come to the third test we began this
paper with, by laying down that the veracity of a
tradition should be held by all, in all places, and at
all times.

One of the most apparent instances of this is, if we
find some old building which, either falsely or not,
has been the shrine of some person's name for a very
long period, going back as far as we can judge, to that
period when that person lived. What we wish our
reader to understand, much as it might be desired if it
were so, is, it does not ruin the inference if that
building be genuine or not if it has always been
considered as belonging to, and named after, the
person with whom it is associated, for if so, it is a very
great factor in handing on a veritable tradition.
Take, for instance, the house still shown to the
traveller as the house of the Virgin at Nazareth,
though there is a rival house shown in Italy at Loretto
—and one of the two must be false—still both testify
to the existence that once at Nazareth a person dwelt
there called Mary the Virgin. At Glastonbury, from
a very early time, the ancient church of wood and
wicker, reared on British soil to the honour of Christ,
was preserved as a hallowed relic even after a greater
church of stone was built by Saxon Dunstan to the
east of it. This wooden church originally was
dedicated by Joseph and his companions to the

Blessed Virgin (see Cressy, bk. 2, ch. 7, and " Monast. Angl.," i, p. 2, and Fuller's " Church Hist.," ii, p. 13), but soon became known as the Chapel of St. Joseph. Now we ask the reader if Joseph was never at Glastonbury, why was it known as his chapel from then up to the present day—and why, unless those early converts looked on Joseph as the bringer of their Faith, had his name the singular excellence bestowed upon it of being substituted in this little church for the Blessed Virgin?

Pertinent to this inquiry another of great moment, as it seems to the writer, arises in this controversy— why should Joseph of Arimathea's name at all be handed down as the first bringer of Christianity to Britain if he never came?

And here we think it well to confute a rather popular argument for the saint's coming to Britain, because a false defence is worse than none at all. It engenders suspicion in other defences which may, or are, perfectly legitimate. We refer to the argument which has been used by some to show Joseph introduced Christianity first into Britain from the fact that when St. Austin arrived on his mission to Saxon England he found in what was left of the ancient British Church, variants in their manner of tonsure, keeping Easter, etc., to those then obtaining among the Western nations of Europe—and specially of Rome. The argument, therefore, has been that these variants in custom are Eastern, and were brought from the East by Joseph.

We will only point out if Joseph came to Britain

about A.D. 63-64 the tonsure as unknown then, and for some time to come, anywhere in the Church. Much later we find St. Jerome deprecating eccentricity in this respect, and expressing his dislike to both long hair and shaven heads. The fourth Council of Carthage merely forbids clerics to wear long hair; therefore, as tonsure was unknown when Joseph is said to have arrived here, this variant of it cannot be attributed to him. As to Easter, the difference between Western and Eastern usage in A.D. 63-64 did not exist. It was only nearly a hundred years after Joseph that St. Polycarp came to Rome and to his surprise found two dates for celebrating Easter.

From all this can be seen that it is a feeble argument to bring forward these variant usages to prove Joseph came to Britain, they might just as well be put down to St. Philip or another Apostle, for indeed if being of Eastern origin they think such trace back to Joseph, as he came from the East, why not to the great Apostles, for they were all from, and of, the East?

But why is it necessary to thus bolster up this most ancient tradition? From the earliest ages this place of Glastonbury has been looked on as peculiarly holy, and if so, why? For other of our abbeys have had saints for their founders; other abbeys holy memories and shrines. It could only arise because from a continuous tradition that Joseph of Arimathea first founded it. So, in those ages, it was to them something more than Netley and Tintern, Rievaulx and Fountains.

It was in its own special aspect something more even than the royal minster of St. Peter, the crowning place of Harold and William. It stood out distinct even among the great and venerable foundations of Saxon birth, which were already great when the country fell into the hands of the Normans. Here and here alone on English soil we are linked not only to the beginnings of English Christianity, but of Christianity itself. The rich sweet perfumes of the spices of Arimathea seem here pervading the air, the two white angels of the rock-hewn sepulchre walk its long aisles, and the venerable man who once prepared his Lord for burial finds his own here. Here, too, in all probability, the twelve disciples of St. Philip, sent by him under the leadership of Joseph, for the most ancient annalists say they sojourned here for nine years, but here assuredly many of their disciples who, in imitation of them, led a hermit's life, until to them came St. Patrick, the great Apostle of the Irish and first abbot of this hallowed spot. Here, too, came St. Benen, the disciple of St. Patrick, here St. Gildas, the historian of the British, here, St. David, here the holy hermit Indractus with his seven companions, all of the royal race. All these and many others here chose to live and die. Why? Well, their doing so answers that question—they believed the truth of the story that here once lived he who had been the blessed saint who had tended in his lonely death the Crucified Lord of Glory. There could, and can be, no other reason.

So, too, in later centuries, even from far distant Northumberland, there were brought here to Avalon the relics of Paulinus and of Aidan and Ceolfoid, of Boisel, of Benet Biscop.

"Now I do not ask you" (writes a modern historian) "to believe there was some special cause why legends of this kind should grow in such a shape and in such abundance round Glastonbury alone of all the great monastic churches of Britain, unless the glorious tradition of its first founder had not been recognized and believed in as a great handed-down and historical fact by all these historical saints themselves."

No wonder when Dunstan, as a boy, was led here on pilgrimage, he saw, as in a dream, an aged man clothed in snowy vesture leading him through the simple and then half-ruinous chapels, and that that dream, in waking and in sleeping, should come to so many. After that this place, for memory of that old man, gained through the later Middle Ages the epitaph of " Roma Secunda."

In such great reverence was the church and church-yard held that the compiler of " The Monasticon " (vol. i. p. 17) tells us that " our forefathers did not dare to use any idle discourse or spit therein without great necessity(!). Enemies and wicked men were not suffered to be buried therein, neither did any bring any horse, hawk or dog. For if they did, it was observed they immediately died thereupon. The church by its antiquity was by the old English called Eald Church, and the men of those days had no oath more sacred and formidable than to swear by this old church."

Now why we quote this from " The Monasticon "
(though it evidently, from the time it was written, was
long subsequent to Joseph's alleged arrival in
Britain) is to ask the reader if this ultra-sacredness that
Glastonbury was then held in did not arise from the
conviction that the presence of this first missionary,
and his probable burial there, made its pre-eminent
sanctity?

Other abbeys and other churches at the time " The
Monasticon " was compiled possessed royal founders
and relics of saints; others possessed long lists of
abbots and saintly brothers buried in their garths, but
none could, like Glastonbury, boast they had, as the
initial founder of that monastic settlement, he who had
anointed the dead Body of Christ and handled the
Crucified.

Again, pertinent to this it may be asked why—if
not for this reason—all through the Middle Ages
great pilgrimages were made thither, and that not
only of our own countrymen, but of foreigners
beyond sea?

Judging by analogy—as such famous cosmopolitan
pilgrimages were during that period made to the
shrines of Thomas of Canterbury and of Edward the
Confessor at Westminster, where in both cases their
presence in the flesh had been, and after death their
bodies were entombed, and which were the objects of
their pilgrimages—is it not most reasonable to think
that their other great pilgrimages to far-off Glastonbury were made in a like sure belief of those ages that
Joseph, the founder of the Christian Faith in England,

N

might there be sought for by their prayers, and that his
holy body they believed was there buried, in the same
way as the Confessor's at Westminster, and Becket's
remains at Canterbury?

Again, the renewed building of this church and its
surroundings by the early Saxon kings and those
following, all shows a belief they had in this great
tradition.   As, for instance, King Ina, Cedwall's
successor.   In the year 708 he demolished all the
building that was ruinous and built the abbey almost
new, "and this was the fourth time of its building.
The first time being at the first planting of Christianity
by St. Joseph of Arimathea.   The second by St.
David, Archbishop of Menevia, which being again run
to ruin, was raised up again by twelve well-affected
men of the north.   The great abbey this king (Ina)
here built anew . . . one of the chapels which I take
to be St. Joseph's, he garnished over with gold and
silver and gave to it ornaments and vessels likewise
of gold and silver " (Speed's " Chronicle," p. 228,
and Sammess' " Antiquities," p. 568, and Camden's
" Britannia," Somersetshire).

Therefore, as a modern writer well says : " The
wooden church of the Briton is represented by the
Lady Chapel, better known as the Chapel of St.
Joseph; the stone church of the West Saxon (Ina) is
represented by the vast abbey church itself.   Nowhere
else can we see the works of conqueror and the conquered thus standing, though but in a figure, side by
side.   Nowhere else among all the churches of
England can we find one which can thus trace up an

uninterrupted being to the days before the Teuton had set foot upon British soil. It stands alone among English minsters as the one link which really does bind us to the ancient church of the Briton and the Roman " (see " Origin of English Nation," by E. E. Freeman, in *Macmillan's Mag.*, May, 1870.

We mentioned (*supra*) the tradition and firm belief held in the early Middle Ages that St. Joseph's body was buried at Glastonbury, and this seems to be borne out (besides the notorious facts we have given of pilgrimages and kings' offerings here in his honour for many centuries) by the fact in the list given in " The Monasticon " of relics preserved at the abbey; varied and strange were many such, as some of the teeth of St. Peter, some of our Lord's hair, and many other fraudulent relics—*no single relic is mentioned* as that of St. Joseph whom the monks of that period (when relic-hunting and collecting was both a profitable trade and a mania) would, in ordinary cases, have placed there in that list. Now such relics are never mentioned among those displayed in reliquaries on altars if the whole body of a saint is known to be entire, and known to be buried in a certain place, particularly when that burial place has been a place of notoriety for long centuries of belief. Therefore, from this absence of relics of their own acknowledged founder, we think it a very fair inference to draw that the body of Joseph of Arimathea was known by a continual tradition to rest in the sacred ground of the abbey of Glastonbury in Avalon.

Believing this, an old English poet exclaims :

" Heyle, tresour of Glastonbury moost imperyall
In savour smellynge swete as eglantyne
Now shall thy name flourysshe ouerall
Jhesu for thy sake the bell of mercy doth rynge."
     (Written by unknown author, temp. *Henry VII.)*

This firm belief, from the date of these lines,
temp. Henry VII, will show had gone on through all
the ages since A.D. 63-64.   Even later than this date,
in the reign of Mary Tudor, we find the monks who
had been dispossessed by her father, Henry VIII,
praying her for their restoration to this earliest home
of Christianity in Britain.

To sum up, it has been shown from the foregoing
that this tradition of St. Joseph of Arimathea being
the first to preach Christianity in Britain, and resident
at Glastonbury, and being after buried there fulfils the
three tests laid down in the commencement of this
paper as elements, if found, for the acceptance of its
truth by (1) having an element of reasonable
probability; (2) not running counter to any known
historical fact; (3) received in the past by all men, in
all places, and at all times.

Before ending this paper we conceive it would not
be suitably finished unless something was said about
the flowering thorn tree which, for many long centuries,
flourished at Glastonbury, particularly as it may
appear to some—which I do not myself believe—that
its frequent blossoming at Christmas might have been
only from a freak of Nature, or its possibly sheltered

position from winter blasts. The story is well known how the weary and aged Joseph, sitting down for rest on a hill, where afterwards the abbey should be raised, planted his walking-staff in the ground, which took root and grew up a tree, and for long, each winter, flowered about Christmas.

Now first we will remind the reader many other holy men have been credited with something very similar. In the Old Testament we have Aaron's rod flowering before the Egyptian magicians. The legend of St. Boniface, the missionary of Germany, says he planted his staff also in the ground when about to consecrate a church : after it was consecrated the dry staff put forth leaves. So, too, in like manner the staff of St. Bernard planted became a tree (Bolland, 20 March). A medieval traveller recounts on his journey to Smyrna he saw a cherry tree in blossom which was said originally to have been the staff of St. Polycarp. For some time an oak was pointed out at Assisi as sprung from the staff of St. Francis (" Missora Voyage en Italie," vol. iii).

However, certain other saints are in art represented with their staves in their hands, some flowering, some not, which differ from those instances cited above, as remaining staves and not growing into trees they were thus figured for symbolical reasons, as St. Bridget, as a sign at her virginity, so St. Joseph—foster-father of our Lord—to symbolize a like virtue. Now it is apparent to the reader that these cases of rods planted and then turning into trees, in the three cases we have cited—St. Boniface, St. Polycarp, and St. Francis—

whether grown and preserved by a miracle, or surviving because sheltered from adverse climatic changes, prove at the time they existed the holy persons to whom their origin was assigned lived in those places at some time or other—in a word, these trees were silent witnesses that at some period or another in the place they grew, the saint to whom they were for had been there—and this indeed was so, for St. Boniface, the missionary of Germany, we know founded the church of Grossvargnes, where his staff was said to turn into leaf (" Theil," bk. i, p. 342), and was present at its consecration.   St. Polycarp was at Smyrna, St. Francis lived at Assisi; is it therefore an unwarrantable assertion to make by the argument of " ceteris paribus " that the thorn tree at Glastonbury demonstrates that Joseph had indeed been there?   Why otherwise for countless centuries was it identified with him and him alone, and why, if it was a false identification, was it not identified with the great St. Patrick who we know once was there, or with St. Dunstan, or some royal founder such as King Ina?   That this identification was kept up through centuries, for this is, we will again quote the curious poem reprinted by Richard Pynson in the year 1520, showing at all events then (1520) he could point out the thorn as then existing, and bound up in the life of Joseph.   He says:

> " Lo, lordes, what Jhesu dooth in January
>   When the great colde cometh to grounde;
>   He maketh the Hauthorne to sprynge full fresshely
>   Where as it pleaseth hym his grace is founde."
>   (" Lyfe of Joseph of Arimathea," p. 49.)

Now granted that the thorn tree owed its existence not miraculously to Joseph's staff taking life, and that its flowering at Christmastide was owing to either a sheltered spot or some peculiarity in its germs, and that this saintly missionary simply planted some little sapling from the adjoining forest to mark his place of rest, all this in no way will militate against the argument we have drawn from it, that this tree known as Joseph's for long centuries shows he was once there himself where it grew.

But if we grant it was, as the tradition says, indeed from Joseph's staff, and that frequently each year it has blossomed in mid-winter—well, if we believe that Christianity is true and the words of its Founder were true, and that Founder was the Creator and Law-giver of all the natural world, then that such a miracle should take place, and at the time it first occurred, is not unworthy of our credence.   Those wild Britons to whom the gospel was first preached could only be appealed to by the testimony of their eyes.   No learned books of controversy in those days could prove to them the claims of Christianity—even in much later ages it needed images of the holy ones, and their glowing figures on painted glass to be for the unlettered their unwritten Bibles.   It is no wonder, therefore, up and down Europe and Asia during the first preaching of the apostles and of the saints are found, according to the great promise of their divine and absent Founder, miracles wrought and believed in in all good faith.

It was only the frauds perpetrated so often after-

wards by gain-seeking abbots and monks that gradually turned people from believing in any post-
apostolic miracles at all, whereas we know, as the
agnostic scientist Huxley says, " many of these
ecclesiastical miracles rest on as good proofs as many
of those recorded in the orthodox scriptures," and
he elsewhere writes his wonder that those seeking
Christian evidences do not use more the evidences
afforded by miracles, and that miracles are conceivable
and not intrinsically absurd is easily shown.

A little later than this poem—in 1535—Dr.
Layton, sent by the infamous agent of Henry VIII,
Thomas Cromwell, to inspect the monasteries of
Somerset, writes to him on the 24th August from
Bristol: " By this bringer I send you relicks; first, two
flowers wrapped in black sarsnet that in Christmas
Mass even ' Hora ipsa qua Christus natus fuerat ' will
spring in burgen and bare blossoms."

Later still, Sir Charles Sedley, the noted wit of
Charles II's reign, sings in one of his lyrics:

> " Cornelia's charms inspire my lays
> Who fair in nature's scorn,
> Blooms in the winter of her days
> Like Glastonbury thorn."

Much later, down to our own time, a resident at
Glastonbury tells the present writer: " I have lived at
Glastonbury nineteen years, and during that time the
[thorn] tree has failed to blossom at Christmas on
two occasions, one being last Christmas [1921]."

It is granted by most men that God is infinitely
powerful and free. If He is infinitely powerful He

certainly can produce effects in corporeal things which no created activity left to itself could produce in the circumstances; and if He is infinitely free He cannot be said to have been necessitated from eternity so to order the course of created activities as to leave no room for his own immediate interference further than was necessary for the continuance of the world. Miracles, even one to make a dry rod bloom for centuries, are consequently conceivable as works of the Creator's absolute power.

But whether this blossoming thorn owes its strange manifestations of age and flowering to a miracle, or some peculiarity in its genus, alters nothing in its value to us who test the ancient tradition of Joseph's sojourn or not at Glastonbury; its value being this, that from remote ages up to the present day it has by countless persons, noble and simple, been inseparably bound up with the Arimathean, and never with any of the other saintly men who once dwelt in this famous place, therefore a witness to the tradition of Joseph once being there. It is a living testimony in wood, if not in stone, of that continuous belief.

It may be of interest to note that the original tree that had flourished so many centuries was cut down by one of the soldiers in Cromwell's army during the Civil War of King Charles and the Parliament—but a slip of it was re-planted, which now is the thorn tree still seen at Glastonbury in its ancient primal vigour —the heir of a great inheritance!

THE KING'S HEALING

IT may be as well, before entering into this curious subject, and little known at the present day, though well known to our ancestors, to clear the ground, removing an explanation for these cures by the royal touch which otherwise to readers might suggest itself.

In these days, owing doubtless to the greater proficiency in medical science, it has conclusively been proved that the brain, in many obscure diseases, if stimulated, acts in a curative way. Thus, in nervous affections in cases where the limbs have become useless, excitation of the patient's will power or hypnotic suggestion or a roused faith have produced, and still do, remarkable results.

There is little doubt but that many cures in the past, even those which our ancestors attributed to saintly power and relics, owed their origin and efficacy to this now well-known excitation of the mind over the body, and so over all nervous complaints and those allied to them. Hence the so-called " cures " of Christian Science, hence those of so-called " faith-healing." But if the disease is one that cannot be removed by nervous excitation no such result obtains. Now the disease called scrofula, which the king's touch cured, is not of a nervous origin, or to be removed by any will or faith power. An eminent recent-day London physician writes anent this: "Scrofula now recognized as a tubercular disease cannot be affected or cured by any action of the nerve-powers or hypnotic suggestion, or so-called faith healing."

Therefore it follows that these thousands of cures affected by our ancient kings and those of France— as no medicines were used, and children often were cured immediately in the king's presence—must have had their efficacy in some supernatural and miraculous power.

During the reigns of the Stuarts, and far back in the times of the Tudor and Plantagenet dynasties, there was a universal belief, founded on experience, that the royal touch "healed" scrofulous persons, a belief which was also in the latter years of the Stuarts regarded as one of the sure tests of a sound Royalist.

This miracle-working power was assumed to be deposited solely in the persons of the kings of England and France; in England a gift descended to his posterity from St. Edward the Confessor; in France from either a gift of the sacred vase of Chrism by St. Remy to Clovis, or else from the Crusading King, Louis IX.

As regards these counter claims of Clovis and St. Louis, Laurentino ("De Mirabile Stroumas," Paris, 1609), first physician of Henry IV of France, asserts the power of the royal touch to have commenced with Clovis (481), and that Louis probably added to the ceremony. Mezeray bears this out and says,

" through humility, he first added the sign of the Cross when he touched."

As far as England is concerned, all ancient writers have ascribed this gift of healing to have come from Edward the Confessor; it is only in later days a theory has been set up which assumes it to the English sovereigns through the inter-marriage of Edward II with Isabelle of Valois, and so of French origin.

The belief of its English origin Shakespeare, in " Macbeth," has shrined :

> " *Malcolm:* . . . Comes the king forth, I pray you?
> *Doctor:* Ay, sir; there are a crew of wretched souls
> That stay his cure: their malady convinces
> The great assay of art; but at his touch—
> Such sanctity hath heaven given his hand—
> They presently amend. . . .
> *Macduff:* What's the disease he means?
>   'Tis call'd the evil:
> A most miraculous work in this good king;
> Which often, since my here-remain in England,
> I have seen him do."

From the time of our Henry II we find numbers " touched " for this disease; it was not, however, till the reign of Henry VI, that definite regulations and a ritual service were drawn up for the ceremonies of " touching for the King's evil." Then, for the first time, a gold " angel," a coin struck by Henry VI, was, after the royal touch, suspended round the neck of the sick person.

Henry VIII does not seem to have " touched," but Elizabeth used this power, and towards the end of her reign the ancient service was translated into English from the Latin.

James, on succeeding to the English throne, caused considerable anxiety to his ministers for refusing at first to hold these services, but yielded at length, probably for political reasons, to show he was descended from the Confessor (Edward).

But when we arrive at the reign of his son, Charles I, we find in the State Paper Office no less than eleven proclamations issued relating to the royal cure of this evil. One of the earliest fixes the times the king will touch; another orders all that repair to his presence first to get certificates of honesty and also suffering from scrofula from the local magistrates and clergy. The tenth proclamation, after a long abeyance on account of the plague, fixes the dates again of Easter and Michaelmas when the king will touch. It is related of Charles I (Lecky's "Hist.," vol. i., p. 64) that when he was in the hands of the Parliament on his way from Hurst Castle to Windsor as a prisoner, in passing through Winchester an innkeeper there threw himself on his knees and prayed the king to heal him of the evil he suffered from. The king could not, surrounded by guards, "touch" him, but cried out, "God bless thee and grant thee thy desire," thereupon the man was immediately cured.

In the succeeding reign of Charles II this practice assumed great proportions. People flocked from the country to the palace of Whitehall. On the 23rd of June, 1660, no less than six hundred were "touched" by the king. On 16th July of the same year two

hundred more, and there were still a thousand more
waiting to be received (*Parliamentary Intelligencer*,
23rd July, 1660).

In the summer of 1662 the healing services were
fixed and regulated by royal decree.   The King's
sergeant-surgeon was directed to examine into the
bona-fide complaints of all before being admitted to
the King's touch.   The old service of the healing was
read by either a bishop present or the King's almoner
or chaplains.

Lord Macaulay reckons up in his " History " (vol.
iii) that as many as a hundred thousand persons in all
were " touched " by Charles II during his twenty-five
years' reign, and that the cost of the annual ceremony
was not less than £10,000.

Upon James II succeeding to the throne he held
a service of healing at Winchester Cathedral; he also
touched eight hundred persons in the choir of Chester
Cathedral when in that city, and after his flight to
France held various " healings " at St. Germains-en
Laye, where many resorted to him to be touched.

Both his son (James III and VIII) and his grandsons (Charles Edward and Henry) " touched " for the
king's evil.   Prince James, when in Paris in 1716, is
said on excellent testimony to have cured a young
man named Christopher Lovell who travelled all the
way from Bristol to obtain the royal touch.

In the recent life of the Grosvenor family, Lady
Grosvenor, wife of the then baronet of that family, is
stated, on her return from Italy through France, to
have had her son touched by King James for the evil.

Prince Charles Edward, when in the '45 at Edinburgh, " touched " several persons at Holyrood Palace, while Henry, when afterwards he succeeded to his *de jure* rights at the death of his brother, " touched " for the King's evil at Rome—and some of his " touch pieces," or medals, are still extant.

One of the charges against the Duke of Monmouth, illegitimate son of Charles II, was for usurping the royal right of " touching." In a collection of tracts in the British Museum there is a letter from Crewkerne in Somersetshire, and from many others, certifying the miraculous cure of a girl named Elizabeth Parcet, who had been ill with this disease over twelve years, and as Monmouth rode by she seized his bare wrist and pressed it to her sores, and on her return home shortly she was perfectly healed. This is signed by her minister and witnesses, and seems perfectly genuine.

Turning to the kings of France:

Louis XI in the fifteenth century " touched " freely and continually for the evil. On Wolsey's embassy to Francis I that king, on his way to the banquet which he gave to the English embassy, " touched " great numbers of sick people. Philip of Valois is said to have cured fourteen hundred people afflicted with the evil. Of Louis XIII it was said at the time " he had assigned all his powers as king to Cardinal Richelieu except that of curing the King's evil."

Gemelli, the traveller, states that Louis XIV touched sixteen hundred persons on Easter Day, 1686.

The words he used were " Le Roy te touche, Dieu te guerisse." Louis XVI, after his coronation in 1755, "touched" two thousand sick of the evil in the cathedral of Rheims. Even away from France (as our own kings in exile) the King of France exercised this power, for Pierre Desrey in his " Great Chronicle of Charles VIII " says: " Tuesday the 20th the King heard Mass in the French chapel [Naples], and afterwards touched and cured many afflicted with the King's evil to the great astonishment of the Italians who witnessed the miracle."

Even when suffering ill-health the French kings seem not to have been forgetful of their gift of healing, for Philip de Comines, speaking of Louis XI's illness at Forges, near Chinon, in March, 1480, says: " After two days he recovereth his speech and his memory after a sort . . . he had not much to say for he was shriven not long before, because the kings of France use always to confess themselves when they touch those that be sick of the King's evil, which he never failed to do once a week. If other Princes do not the like they are to blame, for continually a great number are troubled with that disease."

To turn to the rival theories whether this miraculous gift of healing came to our English kings by an hereditary power transmitted to them by St. Edward the Confessor, or the more modern theory from the kings of France by the marriage of Edward II with Isabelle of Valois:

(1) It seems to the writer that this French claim

is completely refuted by the fact that the French
kings have always laid their claim on this miraculous
healing power coming to them from the Chrism
contained in the vessel given to, and used by,
St. Remy at the coronation of Clovis (496), and this
gift confirmed to them afterwards by St. Marcoul,
abbot of Nauteil (552), and not from being heirs of
Clovis. In a word, their powers came from each
king being anointed by a miraculous Chrism, and that
it was an individual consecration, and not one that a
woman of their royal house, such as Isabelle de Valois,
could convey as if an hereditary possession to another,
and to a foreign race of kings as the English ones were.

(2) On the other hand, this gift of healing was
never claimed by the English kings to have come
from their anointing. On the contrary, we find in the
household books of Henry IV no miraculous ointment
was ever used, for money is stated to be given to
certain persons to prepare it of herbs and balms for
his coronation, and this seems always the usual
English custom. For instance, later, James II, in
items of his coronation expenses, is found to have given
to his apothecary £200 to prepare ointment for his
sacring.   Again, we find later his descendants, the
de jure James III and VIII, and his grandsons,
Charles Edward and Henry, all " touching " for the
evil and performing cures, and yet these princes had
never been crowned, and certainly not anointed.

One curious fact seems to point, perhaps, to some
belief in the French connection with the English royal
touch.   It is this: Heylin, in his " Cosmograph "

o

(p. 184), says in the chapel of St. Maclou at St. Denys the kings of France, after a fast of nine days and other penances, used to receive the gift of healing; and the historian Carte says, in his " History of England " (vol. i, ch. iv), that to the church of Corbigny in Champagne, where the relics of St. Marculf were preserved, these French kings immediately after their coronation used to go, and, according to some French writers, to obtain from these relics and this saint their power of healing.　Now—and this is a curious thing in connection with the French claim, i.e., that their kings gave this gift to our English ones—in England there was a room in the palace of Westminster, frequently mentioned in the Rolls of Parliament, which was called " The Chamber of St. Marculf," being very possibly the place where our kings anciently touched for the evil. (But might not this chamber have been dedicated to St. Marculf by Edward III or Henry V to bring their claim to be rightful kings of France prominently before their English subjects?)

Again this seems curious if the Norman kings of England gained the touch from the marriage of Henry I with the Saxon kindred of the Confessor, that line in Scotland who sat on the Scottish throne never seem to have claimed or exercised this miraculous inheritance.

Perhaps the earliest and the most valuable testimony to the Confessor's gift is that of Peter of Blois, chaplain to King Henry II, who attests both Henry's power of touching for the evil and the cures ensuing it. And it is valuable for this reason that as none of the former Norman kings " touched," it was only evidently because of Henry II's mother being of Saxon kin to the Confessor, and it being known at that time and recognized that the Confessor was the medium and *fons* of that miraculous gift that Henry did so.

Matthew Paris, who states the Confessor had and transmitted this gift to his descendants, did not, it is true, live in that saint's lifetime; nor, indeed, do two other early chroniclers, but Paris lived near enough to have learnt the universal belief of the period. Again, a very rare poem has lately been unearthed and is invaluable testimony of this belief in Henry III's time. We here quote some parts of it, embodying the miraculous cures effected by Edward the Confessor's touch.

First, it is well to say that this poem is dedicated to " Alianore, riche Reine d'Engleterre " (Queen of Henry III). The author gives very few hints who he was, but from the fact that Edward the Confessor was his subject, and from the elaborate manner in which he enlarges on everything respecting Westminster, it seems probable he was connected with that abbey, and the only hint he gives of himself is when he speaks of how Edward the Confessor

> *De quor verai e tendre*
> *Ama Seint Pere le apostre*
> *Le suen seigneur e le nostre.*

thus apparently claiming St. Peter as his lord. (It has been published by the Rolls Office.)

On the miracle of touching for scrofula by St. Edward he says:

" A very cruel disease
Had a young and beautiful lady
It took away her happiness and joy,
Tainted and darkened her colours,
In her neck she had bare swellings
Which are usually called Scrofulous."

Maladie mut cruele
A une dame e jovens e bele
Leesce e baudur toli
Culur li teint e esnerie
En col nues glandres out
K'em escrovele numer scout.

" In her sleep she hears a voice
Advising her to seek the king,
She does so and discloses to him the reason,"

and when he hears it,

" As a gentle debonair king,
Grants her request.
He takes water with which he had washed,
Sprinkles the spot that pained her,
Strokes the swellings and the sores
Which are foul with disease,
And gently washes them with the water,
Now lo the malady departs."

Cum gentily reis debonaire
Sa request fet aveire;
Del cue prist, dunt out lavé
Le liu doillant ad arusé

L'emfié e boces manie
Ki ord sunt de la maladie,
E ducement del eue leve.
Atant esvus li mans s'escrevé.

The writer ascribes the power to God as a gift to the Confessor:

" For there is no medicine so powerful and life-giving
So sure and so speedy
As is that of Heaven.
When it descends upon mortals
And sick cure.

.   .   .   .

God gives aid to his vassals
By the prayer of St. Edward."

Ke n'est nule si forte e vive
Si seure u si hastive
Cum est mescine du cel
Quant decent sur le mortel:
E li malade garaisun;

.   .   .   .

Fait Deus a ses feus aie
Par le prière Seint Aedward.

I will now cite a few passages from old writers substantiating the claims of St. Edward the Confessor as possessed, and handing down this gift to his posterity.

Jeremy Taylor (" Eccles. Hist. of Great Britain," vol. i, p. 225) says: " That Edward cured the evil is beyond dispute, and since credit of the miracle is unquestionable, I see no reason why we should scruple to believe the rest." He then quotes as his authority

William of Malmesbury, and goes on to explain the nature of the disease, and adds: " King Edward the Confessor was the first that cured this distemper, and from him it has descended as an *hereditary* miracle upon all his successors." William of Malmesbury relates several miracles performed by the Confessor (" De Gestis Regum Anglorum "), one of which refers to a woman afflicted with the evil and who, being admonished in a dream to seek the royal touch, entered the palace when the king " touched " her and complete health followed. According to the same authority Edward, before being a king, had previously cured this evil in Normandy (" multotiens cum in Normannia hanc pestem sedasse ferunt, qui interius epis vitam novercent "). In the " Computus Hospitii " of Edward I (preserved in the Record Office) a small gold medal as given by the Confessor to those he touched for the evil is frequently mentioned. John of Gaddesden, who flourished in 1320, of Merton College, Oxford, extolled by Chaucer as the then most illustrious writer on medicine, refers to the royal touch—after enumerating various treatment for scrofula, if they fail he advises sufferers to repair to the king, " Si hæc non sufficiant vadat ad Regem ut eum tangat atque benedicat."

Bradwardine, Archbishop of Canterbury, who lived in the reign of Edward III and Richard II, dying in 1348, gives his testimony to the antiquity of the practice, and appealing to its truth, says: " Quicumque negas miracula Christiane, veni et vide ad oculum." Sir John Fortescue, Chief Justice in the time of

Henry IV, and afterwards Chancellor to Henry IV, represents the privilege of touching for the King's evil as a practice from time immemorial belonging to the kings of England. Polydore Vergil (*temp.* Henry VII and VIII) directly describes it as a gift from St. Edward the Confessor " quod quidam immortale munus jure quasi hæreditario ad postiores reges manavit, nam reges Angliæ etiam hunc tactu ac quibusdam hymnis non sine cæremoniis prius recitalis, strumosos sanant " (" Hist Angliae," bk. xxii, p. 187).

This is an important testimony, as it describes this gift of touching as an hereditary one, and from the Confessor.

In a MS. in the University Library of Cambridge in a memorandum (" Ant. Mirac.," p. 384) which says, " The kings of England and Fraunce by a peculiar guift cure the kynge's Evil by touching them with their handes and soe doth the seventh child."

Dr. Tucker, Chaplain to Queen Elizabeth, in his work " Charismate " denies that the kings of France originally cured the evil, but " per aliquam propaginem," i.e., by an offshoot of right derived from the primitive power of the English kings under whose jurisdiction so much of France was held by the Angevin dynasty.

A much later historian of our own times (Professor G. S. Phillips, of Ushaw) states: " St. Edward the Confessor was the first king of England to touch for the King's evil—many sufferers from which disease were cured by him." From all this evidence the claim of France to have brought this gift to our

English kings must fail, for it shows long before the marriage of Richard with Isabel.

(1) Now without pronouncing on the validity or not of many cures said to have been performed by the saints or their relics in days gone by—still every one will acknowledge many of these, perhaps the greater part, took place in isolated places—sacred shrines and churches—where the validity of the cures were seen and possibly (?) tested by comparatively few onlookers.

These cures, on the other hand, effected by the royal touch were in open court, in palaces, and cathedrals, before great multitudes of people; tested when the cures took place, by the best physicians of the day, and recorded, most particularly, by the annalists of the time, who certainly, in the time of the Stuart dynasty, were very loath to give to royalty its prerogatives of either honours or subservience.

(2) Again, this power of the royal touch—as far as our English sovereigns—had this peculiarity, it did not seem to confine its efficacy to the goodness inherent in the one who touched, nor in her or his legitimate right to exercise it—Henry IV, V and VI were usurpers. Henry VII was so likewise. Mary or Elizabeth (whichever view their father's divorce from Katherine of Aragon is held by readers) was, one of them, a bastard: Anne, a usurper of her father's throne. Yet all these touched for the King's evil, and Anne particularly held solemn and stated intervals to do so, and her cures were substantiated by well-known doctors,

As to morality or saintly lives neither Elizabeth nor Charles II nor Monmouth were famed for such— Charles, who touched successfully more than any king before, was notorious for his sensual life, yet all these participating in a few drops in their veins of St. Edward's blood, performed these miraculous cures.

With one or two exceptions (turning to their rival miracle-workers in France) the same strange unsaintly lives present themselves to the reader in history. If Edward III's contention was right (and later historians in considering his claims to the French crown, hold, not a few, that he was justified) then from that time they were all usurpers; at all events, many princes of the houses of Valois and Bourbon were blemished with great lapses in virtue—and few morally fitted to have been worthy to hold this gift of healing bestowed by St. Remy, yet they both had it, and exercised it freely, and, from excellent testimony of the days in which they lived, successfully.

If any reader asks for an explanation of this strange " gift," unless a miraculous origin is given for it, there seems now as far as ordinary medical science helps, none whatever. As an Oxford member of that profession a few years ago, writing on the subject, said : " In past times no one appears to have questioned the validity of the means, and no one has attempted to explain the results obtained, but in connection with the sanctity or inherited sanctity of the Prince who touched for the evil, and indeed the *bona-fide* facts given by these happy results and the known complaint they dealt with—scrofula, which unlike some other diseases can be dissipated, or 'healed' by excitement of the nervous system—are still inexplicable unless, as those did who lived when these cures took place, we accept a miraculous reason for their efficacy."

Reviewing the evidence as to the claims of the French and English kings it seems:

(1) Those of France rested for the efficacy of their touch of healing on receiving at their coronation their anointment from the "ampulla," or vase, of such given as tradition has it, by St. Remy to Clovis, the first Christian king of the Franks. Theirs was from their anointing.

(2) Those of England contrawise rest on the miraculous gift bestowed on Edward the Confessor, which appears to have embraced his kith and kin (for he had no children), and from the niece of Edward the Atheling to have descended to his remote posterity.

So theirs was from their hereditary descent.

The sources and channels of this gift differed in the royal families of France and England.

This " descent " from Edward the Confessor must also be used guardedly, for that king had no offspring. His monkish chroniclers rejoice in his vow of celibacy —in using, therefore, the word " descent " rightly it can only be used as a gift from him descending to his kith and kin. We here show the relationship.

Edward the Confessor was only step-uncle in a remote degree of Saxon Edith, wife of Henry I of England, and daughter of Malcolm, King of Scots, and Margaret his wife, sister of Edward the Etheling; but both had a common ancestor in Alfred the Great.

It may be of interest, before ending this paper, to mention the "touch-pieces" which latterly, at the sovereign's healing service, was suspended by him or her round the patient's neck.

It was not till the reign of Henry VII that we find these used; then a beaten coin of about the size of a thin half-crown, made of gold, and called an angel, and first struck by Henry VI, was used. It had on one side St. Michael slaying the dragon, and on the other, a warship with the legend, " A domina factum est et est mirabile in oculos nostros."

Elizabeth reduced the size of the coin, and put as a legend, " Soli Deo Gloria."

Charles II used an even smaller "touch-piece," and we can understand from the thousands he "touched" the necessity of economy in this. The historian Macaulay, as before said, calculates the annual cost during the twenty-five years of his reign amounted to not less than £10,000.

James II, both before and after his flight to France, used even a smaller angel, and the legend " Soli Deo Gloria."

His son and two grandsons used a still further reduced coin, and latterly gave an angel of silver instead of one of gold.

In the British Museum is one of these "touch-pieces " of James VII and VIII.

What is to be said at the conclusion of all this evidence, a great deal from perfectly painstaking persons, and many of them eye-witnesses of these wonderful cures? We have to acknowledge as far as medical science—even of to-day—there is no solution, and if we fall back on the unseen and miraculous, it will have to be acknowledged—considering the character of many of the sovereigns who used it—it was a gift impersonal to the user, and as the legend on the later "touch-pieces" proclaims—"Soli Deo Gloria."

While it was practised by our sovereigns—particularly by Charles II, seeing the numbers who flocked from all parts of the country to his court to be touched, and we are assured who mostly went away healed—it was a very great factor in keeping up a loyal spirit in the kingdom. Wherever these touched people went, they sung his praises, and whatever the personal or political character of the sovereign might be, to them and all who heard of the cures his touch proclaimed he was God's anointed. And this also no doubt was one of the factors that drew men's eyes and often their hearts and swords to the exiled Stuarts, this strange, miraculous gift of healing which in the wide world except with the kings of France rested through, and by, their hands.

The service for the royal healing disappeared from the Book of Common Prayer soon after the death of the last sovereign here who practised it—Queen Anne. It is said, however, to have been found in a rare edition of the Prayer Book published in 1727. Till the time of Elizabeth the service was always in Latin—she had it translated into English. It commenced by reading the first lesson (St. Mark xvi. 14) to "miracles following," during which, according to the rubric at the words " they shall lay their hands on the sick, and they shall recover," the infirm persons are presented to the king on their knees and the king layeth his hands upon them. This was followed by a second lesson (St. John i. first verse to " grace and truth ") during which " they are again presented to the king upon their knees and the king putteth his gold about their necks." Then came certain prayers and responses to be made by those about to be healed, ending with a Collect for God's help and blessing. Thus, as a present-day writer in his own essay on this curious and little-known subject sums up: " Every spring and autumn persons who were victims of this terrible scourge resorted to the presence of their sovereign to have the touch of his sacred hand to cure them of their ills " (F. A. Inderwick, Q.C., in his " Side Lights ").

LEGEND MAKERS

SACRED legends have to be received in many cases with great suspicion. Many are adaptations from the acts and occurrences recorded of others in the Old and New Testaments. Others are grafted on to known historical saints to supply the gifts of others less known, while in nearly all, symbols, originally used for pure mystical teaching of spiritual gifts, have been distorted into fabulous and real things and persons.

Much of these failings arose from the original writers of these legends being perfectly incompetent for true historical research and criticism, or of the right or wrong, of the material they used; other legends again were for the profit of, and exaltation of, the relics supposed to be possessed by some church or monastery, so added to, and, by the monks, embellished, that they might have greater attractions to offer to the constant bands of wandering pilgrims who in the Middle Ages went from one altar to another in many lands; and certainly, and lastly, in some legends, the makers incorporated pagan ones, and in incorporating them gave them, for acceptance, a faint halo of Christianity.

Again, the conception we hold of the Creator as

a being of divine simplicity and unity in all His actions, and of sublime reason, is unlike the conception of these past ages of Him. They thought of Him as one continually altering His laws of nature; on certain occasions a hermit or an anæmic nun could sway His councils; the storms marked His displeasure, the tempests His sudden wrath, and all they saw of anything unusual in their world, they attributed to the marvellous and the miraculous. For instance, Matthew Paris relates in his " Chronicle " both birds and animals had been restored to life at the tomb of Thomas à Becket.

The appeal to man's inner conscience and to the eyes of his soul, in these half primitive ages, was an unknown thing to the multitude—the exterior life, with its passions and sensations, was the only one known to such—it followed, therefore, it was not the beautiful or spiritual in their saints that appealed to them, it was their outward working in some miraculous manifestation, real or feigned. Hence to supply such constant legends of the saints working such, the old monastic chroniclers invented for their people innumerable and unauthentic legends.

Again, the symbolic and parabolic language, being of eastern origin—in which the scriptures were written—helped on this love of taking those narratives which, originally, were to be read as symbolic or allegorical, as literal and mundane facts. " The stars fought against Sisera" the Hebrew poet had sung, but the poetry was turned into a proof that the destinies of human beings were controlled by the stars—the poetical assertion that the sun and moon stood still—in every homily delivered was not a poetic figure, but a real fact. When Moses discovered a stream or well in the desert it was turned into the legend that he found it by striking the hard rock with his staff. The latter was a myth common to the East—in Greek mythology Bacchus with his thrysus strikes the ground and a stream flows forth; and Atalanta thrusts her lance against a rock and the waters gush out.

If we turn to the New Testament we shall find the same bias of these ages turning what were intended as parables or allegorical stories to enforce a moral truth into real facts. Thus the beggar Lazarus is considered to have been a real living person, and as such made the patron of all lazar houses, and the road where the " Good Samaritan " journeyed along, still, in the Middle Ages, was shown to the traveller, though the Samaritan himself had only existed in the parable.

But there was also another useful element at hand for the legend maker—the assimilation of well-known persons or incidents in the Old and New Testaments with those otherwise deficient in their life history. Thus Moses striking the rock was copied into the legend of St. Pol, St. Leufroy, St. Paternus, St. Nicholas, and St. Augustine, and several others. (See " Acta Sanct.," Bolland.)

The feeding of Elijah by ravens was the ground-work of the legends of St. Vitus and Modestus, who were in them figured as fed by an eagle. In the

Chronicle of the Order of Citeaux, when St. Etienne, third of the abbots there, is stated to have been fed by an eagle and a fish, the fabrication is plainly stated whence derived, " from the ravens sent to feed Elijah by the Almighty."

The legacy, by Elijah, of his mantle to Elisha is assimilated into the legend of St. Anthony, the first hermit who received, according to it, the mantle of Athanasius. The smiting of the waters of Jordan by Elisha again has its counterpart in the legend of St. Benoit, another saint—St. Waleue is depicted exactly like Abraham receiving, under disguise, an angel as his guest. Because Aaron's rod is said to have devoured serpents, so St. Pol, Bishop of Leon, and St. Nicholas and St. Augustine did the same. The legend makers could not leave alone the account of the Three Children in the Old Testament, delivered over, and coming safe out of the fiery furnace; St. Victor and St. Maur were both credited with the like fire and safe return (Lenain de Tillemont), and so numerous other saints.

Turning to the New Testament the miraculous deliverance of St. Peter from prison attracted the legend makers to weave the same story round—among many others—St. Saturninus, St. Roch, and St. Apollonius. But it was specially to the Blessed Virgin and her parents the legends ran and multiplied, because the orthodox evangelists were sadly deficient in the information for these legendaries. It was particularly at the period of the Crusades and the platonic loves, fostered by the *trouvères* and

P

troubadours, that the cult of the Virgin so increased. Her son was God, but also man, and the same craving that fostered in pagan days the cult of Isis over the male gods Osiris and Horus, being of the female sex, appealed to those masculine knights and those warrior classes. It was the exaltation of the female over male, and we may suppose, as long as humanity is what it is, the fascination of it will predispose men unduly to exalt this cult, particularly in the south of Europe, once the land of the troubadour, where these tendencies most obtain.

What, therefore, was wanting by the legend makers was far fuller particulars than the meagre accounts of Mary and her parents the compilers of the orthodox gospels had left. To supply these particulars, legends had to be woven, and, even in those ancient scriptures, interpretations never contemplated by the original compilers were introduced. As an instance of this, the account in Genesis of the Creation was assimilated into the legend of Joachim and Anna—the parents of the Blessed Virgin. Christopher de Vega thus explains it—we give it for its subtility:

" God created the heaven and the earth "—that is Joachim and Anna.

" The earth was void and without form "—that was Anna, long sterile and unchildbearing.

" It was watery "—those were the tears of Anna over her sterility.

" The spirit of God moved above the waters "—

that was His spirit moving over and dispelling Anna's tears.

" God said, Let there be light "—that was Anna's birth of the glorious Virgin, her child.

" The waters were gathered together "—that was in Mary, in whom all graces were gathered together.

Again, incidents in the life of Christ were, in the legends, served up as incidents happening to His mother. Thus the Christ, as a child, had been in the temple asking and disputing with the Elders—Mary, in the legends, at three years old, was stated to have done the same.

In one of the Apocryphal writings the account of the Annunciation, found in the orthodox, is calmly taken and assimilated with a like annunciation to Anna and Joachim, of the speedy birth of their daughter Mary—the angel appears to Anna and foretells that in her daughter " all nations of the earth will be blessed." The angel then proceeds to find Joachim, who is feeding his flock, and asks him why he has put away his wife, and he replies, for twenty years he has lived with her and she is childless—in almost the exact words of the angel in the orthodox Gospel the angel commands him to take her back, and that she shall have a child, who shall be above all women blessed.

We find this primal annunciation—originally used to announce to the Virgin the birth of her Son who should work wonders—copied into the legendary births of many of the saints. Thus of St. Bernard (*vie de Saint Bernard*, by St. Thierry), St. Dominic (*vie* by Lacordaire), St. Eligius, and St. Bridget. A voice comes to the mother of St. Clare declaring " To fear nothing for of her is about to be born a daughter, who will be a light unto the world." So, too, a voice is heard by the mother of our own St. Columba, declaring the same graces and gifts will be in her new-born son.

Even in the sixteenth century this assimilation with the life of Christ given by the evangelists was carried on. It is not here disputed—it is acknowledged by both Catholics and Protestants that St. Francis was a noted saint and conformed his spiritual life—as far as a man could—to his Redeemer's, but his life, as such, was not sufficient for legend makers. Bartholomew de Pisa, in his " Liber Aureus," carried on the analogy much further, i.e., Francis's birth was announced by the prophets; that he had twelve disciples; that one (John of Capella) was rejected by him, as Judas was by Christ; that he suffered in temptation by the devil, as Jesus did, and, like Him, put his adversary to flight, and that he was transfigured; that he suffered the same passion as the Saviour. That Francis was patriarch, prophet, apostle, martyr, doctor, confessor, virgin, angel; and another writer says (Raynauld, " De Stigma," p. 209), " So like was Francis to Christ that the Blessed Virgin, his mother, could hardly distinguish which was which."

This constant practice of taking incidents or events in Christ's life and introducing them into the legendary lives of the saints, might be traced out in numerous more incidents than here given. Even the circumstances of, and after, His Resurrection were so utilized.

St. Germain predicted, as Christ had, his own death to his followers (Bolland, " Acta Sancta ") who did not, as Christ's did not, understand what he meant. St. Ambrose (Fleury, " Hist. Eccles.") appeared to a number of saints after his death, with all the circumstances given in the Gospels of Christ's appearances. Saint Maurille showed himself after death as Christ did under the appearance of a gardener (*Giry*, 13 Sept.). St. Peter Pascal is, like St. Thomas, corrected in his infidelity by Christ allowing him to touch his wounds (*Giry*, 23 Oct.).

Sufficient of these examples, however, of the life of Christ being the source of a great many legends worked into the lives of saints, has perhaps been now given; let us turn to another way where the legend makers found material—that by utilizing spiritual gifts and spiritual achievements in men's holy lives for material of actual achievements by such. This method is very similar to the way—which later will be treated of—how spiritual symbols or emblems were thus confused. Two of the most notable instances of the above are the legends interwoven round the well-known saints, Christopher and Nicholas of Myra.

Christopher's original name, that is, as far as the tradition is to be believed, was Offerus. He was a converted pagan and a dweller in Palestine, noted for his fierce temper and strength, and perhaps kept a

boat to ferry people across the river. This is the
simple outline which was in vogue before the legend
makers filled it up with ample details.

The story of Christopher as told is beautifully
poetic. He was a pagan inhabitant of Palestine or
Canaan. A rough rude man of great strength, he
sought to be with a master similar in strength. The
king he served he thought was such till he found that
king feared the sign of the Cross. Wandering afresh,
still in quest of a perfectly fearless master, he met a
hermit who converted him and baptized him to
Christianity, but one night—for he was serving to
ferry people over the river—a child's voice called him
to do so. He took the little child, unknowing his
weight, on his shoulders through the stream, and
found to his amazement he could hardly support the
weight of that child, so great it was. Crying out in
wonder, the child replied, " You carry the weight of
the world upon your shoulders, for I am its Creator,"
so he knew he had ended his quest, and had found a
Master stronger and more powerful than any.

Now originally, woven round probably, a mere
ordinary conversion to Christianity of a then unknown
man, the first legend maker of it, without a doubt,
wished, as by an allegory, to convey some great
spiritual truths—the man's original name, therefore,
was changed to Christopher—" a bearer of Christ "
—according to the admonition of St. Paul, " Portate
Deum in corpore vestro " (1 Cor. vi. 20), and in the
words of St. Prosper, " Bear Christ in your heart as
if a treasure," and also in the words of blessed Ivo

Carnot (*Term de Purif. B. Virg.*): "How can one carry God? To walk in His image, to imitate Christ."

Thus the legend of the Holy Child carried over the river by Christopher was an allegory originally conceived by the first legend makers of the necessity for a Christian to carry in his heart and in his life his Saviour and God.

Again, the river he thus had to pass over, what was it in allegory but a representation of this man Christopher's baptism? So St. Augustine writes, "per mare transitus baptismus est." Here the comparison is not to a river, but the sea—still it is water. So anciently in certain churches in those ages they sang:

"O holy Christopher
Who has carried Christ
Through the Red Sea,"

the Red Sea being frequently, in those ages, taken as a figure of the waters of baptism.

Now, beautiful as the allegory was, the ignorant soon wanted something more than this mystical legend—they desired a material and literal fact. To meet this want, Christopher was made a giant, and actually, and not figuratively, he was said to have carried the Holy Child, not through the allegorical waters of baptism, but through an angry and foaming river of Palestine; and thus spoilt, the legend has come down to our own day.

Turning to the story of Nicholas of Myra, the

same distortion of a beautiful allegory has been handed down to the present time.

On their way to school three little boys were said to have been actually caught by a ferocious man, a giant, who slew them and salted them down in a tub for future food. St. Nicholas, one day travelling, happened to enter the place they were hidden in; he stood above the tub, and by miraculous power restored these three boys to life and health, and rescued them from their oppressor. This is the story carved in many a church and handed down to the present day as a truth.

What spiritually did this allegory originally represent?

It was the resurrection to a new life through the waters of baptism. St. Nicholas, a great missionary bishop, converted three persons whom he found lying dead to spiritual things; the tub in the allegory was the font of baptism which he raised them up from— naked, as in allegory, and still in art, they were, and are; it was to illustrate " naked come we into this world, naked we shall go out of it." It is possible they may have been children, as they are always so depicted in art, but more probably men who in those days were often carved and made smaller than the chief " actor " in the drama, to show their subservience to the latter.

(This form of portraying by smaller figures those depicted with those higher in dignity, can constantly be found in the Middle Ages, as on altar tombs of a man and his family, where the grown-up sons and daughters kneel as quite small figures behind their larger hewn parents.)

A like obliteration of a spiritual resurrection into a literal fact, as the last-named one, is to be found in the legend also of St. René, founded on the literal signification of his name (Renatus). He had lived seven years a life of sin, that is in paganism, when St. Maurille found him and converted and baptized him. But the legend maker asserted he had been raised when literally lying dead, not dead in spiritual, but in human, life, by a miracle of that saint. Thus the Gallican martyrology runs: "St. Renatus postquam mortuus in sepulchro annos septem jacuisset, a St. Maurillio revocatus est ad vitam" (St. Renatus, after being buried seven years, was raised to life of St. Maurille), and if it be objected that this refers to a resurrection of a human life departed, raised again up to life, let it be remembered that baptism was frequently referred to by the Church as a "second birth" and the font as a "lavacrum regenerationis" (a laver of regeneration).

These three instances, that of St. Christopher, St Nicholas, and St. René will give the reader a view of how allegorical and spiritually veiled truths were treated by the legend makers by placing them on a materialistic and literal basis.

The early Christians in the catacombs always, if they used such, adopted emblematic adornments to express spiritual beings or spiritual truths. Thus the lamb for Christ; the fish for the same, representing the letters of His office and name; sometimes even

the emblem of Mercury for the same person; the vine
for Him, being the root and sustenance of the
Church; the dove for the Holy Spirit; the anchor for
Christian hope—these and many others were emblematic of great spiritual truths, but in no sense were
intended to be, or indeed were, taken literally.
Therefore later, when figures of the saints were
gradually introduced, it was a very general practice
to place certain articles in the hand of, or by, their
effigies, but still only to be as emblems of their inner
lives and characters.

However, this higher and purer spirit of allegorical
representation soon the credulity of the people and the
activity of the legend makers not long permitted to
remain such.

These original emblematic signs and figures the
people turned into facts, occurring, they said, in these
different saints' lives. The populace craving for such
materialistic particulars, and the monks who were
adepts at weaving them being only too ready, it is not
to be wondered at that the strange legends of the
Middle Ages became so variant and so copious. The
emblematic figures placed by the four evangelists they
seem to have left in their spiritual significance intact,
i.e., St. Matthew, the man; St. Mark, the lion;
St. Luke, the ox; St. John, the eagle; but not so
others. St. Jerome has a lion beside him—the legend
is made on it that he talked with a lion in the desert—
the spiritual significance lost, that he resisted the
temptations of the spiritual lion. So also the same
figure beside that of St. Emerius, for his overcoming

a lion in the spirit—the legend asserts he literally did
so in the flesh.   This animal also appears in the legend
of St. John the Silent, not for an emblem of overcoming in a spiritual, but in a literal, combat—so in
that of St. Pelagius and of Paul the Hermit.

The figure of a wolf is used in the same way.
Originally placed by the figure of a saint to represent
the Evil One he spiritually had overcome, the legend
was soon made that he literally had met with such.
This was also the case with the bear, also representing
originally the Evil One, but treated afterwards
literally: as in the case of the legends of St. Corbinian,
St. Humbert, St. Maxim, and St. Malo (*Vies des
Saintes de Bretagne*).   For instance, in the legend
of St. Corbinian he is recounted to have been
travelling with his baggage on a pack-horse—the
horse was on the way devoured by a beast—the latter
the saint placed the baggage on, as if a tamed horse,
until he had come to Rome, where he dismissed the
beast.

A dog was also originally placed by some saints'
effigies—the dog again being considered an emblem
of the Evil One, whom spiritually the saint had overcome.   A great many legends (as even now they do
in our own islands) connect dogs with such demon
appearances.   In antiquity the dog was represented
in the pagan cult of Hecaté.   By this figure a dog or
wolf appears by that of St. Vedast, and so in his
legend, the spiritual significance is lost in a literal
fable.

The little pig is not forgotten by the legend

makers. This beast, considered unclean, was spiritually the type of the concupiscence of the flesh—as such it was placed with a bell round its throat, showing vice had been subdued into spiritual servitude by the saint, by the feet of St. Anthony. Its spiritual significance was soon lost in an absurd legend of Anthony making a pig his pet. For the same reason it also appeared by the side, or feet, of St. Theodore, who made a pig carry a heavy clock for him to the Pope.

The spiritual interpretation of several of these animals is summed up in the dialogues of St. Gregory the Great, where he says: " The devil rages as a lion, brays like an ass, hisses as a serpent, and grunts like a pig." But this spiritual conciseness did not suit the legend makers at all.

The stag always attained to a great position in these sacred legends of the Middle Ages. It often was believed to have indicated where relics were buried—also in different ways to have converted a heathen or an evil liver. In a legend of the thirteenth century one is said to have brought milk to St. Anne, when an infant. A stag was made to have shown to King Dagobert where the bones of St. Denys were hidden (" Great Chronicle of St. Denys," bk. v). A stag in the same way indicated where one of the Scottish saints—Kellac—was buried (Bolland, " Acta Sancta," 1 May).

Saint Branchion, a Thuringian, pursued, when a forester, a hind; the latter took refuge in the cell of a hermit, where the hounds refused to follow her or face her protector. This, the legend says, converted Branchion.

Another legend of the stag is still more vivid. Eustace, Master of the Horse to the Emperor Trajan, in chase with others in the forest, was confronted by a stag having, between his antlers, the figure of the Crucified, while from his mouth Christ asked him why he persecuted Him. Thereupon Eustace was ordered by Christ to seek baptism, and hereafter became a great saint (" Leg. Aur.," vol. 91).

This legend is evidently founded on St. Paul's conversion, and nearly a similar legend is woven round the life of St. Hubert.

These legends, depicting real histories in the lives of saints dealing with stags, were, like so many others, made to supply the place of those allegorical lessons they were originally placed at the side or feet of certain saints' figures in the churches to teach.

If it is asked what originally the carvers of these figures of holy men with stags beside them wished thus to represent, it is little doubt it was to testify to all persons that these men, in their lives, had continually aimed at a very heavenly life, ever ruled by that aspiring cry of the Psalmist, " Like as the hart desireth the water-springs, so desireth my soul after Thee, O God."

If the crucifix appears in the carven emblem, originally, it was to typify the truth—men are only converted through the Cross—and of the allegory recounting that the stag was met by a hunter in a forest, to typify the search of a man's soul through the dark places of this world for divine truths.   The stag, too, was ever regarded as the enemy of the serpent, and so the stag became a symbol of Christ—Christ standing (as a stag) near an effigy of a saint showed that the latter, through his life, had always been under divine protection.

If the mystical or allegorical sense of animals had been kept to, as they originally by the early sculptors had been intended to be, instead of expanded into legends announcing material facts, they would have been of salutary teaching.   An example of one such example left untouched by the legend makers is to be found carved on the south door of one of our own Norman churches in this country, that of Barfreston. Here are two bears discussing with evident relish the contents of a hive of honey.   Below is another bear playing on a harp, while a naked human figure is contorting itself to the music with both hands and feet on the ground.   The lesson the sculptor wished mystically to convey was that the devils—the bears —(always representing at this period evil) are moving their human victim to destruction by bodily and sensual delights (Collins' " Symbolism of Animals "). Here is a spiritual allegory untouched, but if a medieval legend maker had monopolized it, we should find this allegory of a man's soul turned into a veritable history that happened probably to some saint who would have been lured by two evil spirits, under the form of bears he met out one day in a forest, to a place of sensual delights and temptations, and if he overcame them, a conquered figure of a bear would be placed by his stone effigy in some church.

There would not be place in this article to enumerate all the other mystical animals placed by different saints, which the credulous afterwards considered, from the legends woven around them, to have lived, wrestled, and been subdued by these saintly athletes—but one, from its frequency, cannot be left out; the dragon, which, from its mention in the Canonical Scriptures as being the personification of the Evil One, became the companion of many saintly effigies. In the writer's knowledge at least fifty saints are associated with this mythical creature, several of them being local saints of Brittany; but in all, the original significance of the dragon as the type of evil being overcome by good has vanished. Here then, too, was a vast field for legend makers—a drama ready for a credulous audience ever moved by the supernatural.

St. Margaret of Antioch is such a subject. Whether her name was taken from " Margarita," " a pearl," or whether her name was the incentive for the story, she is said to have literally subdued in her life a living dragon on whose forehead was a pearl embedded. It is awkward for this legend that long previously Pliny—the Roman historian—mentions in his day a dragon was discovered similarly decorated (Pliny, bk. 37, c. 10). The legend maker produced the following story for her cult: Her father was a heathen priest of Antioch, but she was brought up by a Christian nurse, whose sheep she used to tend. One day the governor of Antioch saw her, and being captivated by her looks, he ordered her to be taken to his palace, where he desired to take her as his wife. She refused, and he put her to terrible tortures, where she was immured in a dungeon. Here she was tempted by Satan under the form of a dragon, which finally swallowed her up! But the dragon instantly burst asunder, and the saint emerged alive—whereupon she was beheaded by order of the governor.

Henceforth we can see, when this fable was common in Europe, that the original fact of a real saint having subdued by her holy life evil, represented by an allegorical dragon at her feet, was turned into a ridiculous fable of literal fact.

St. Martha of Tarascon had the figure of a dragon placed by her image—originally placed there to again demonstrate how, by a righteous life, she had subdued the evil in and round her. The legend makers came to work, and she was said to have bound captive with her garter a dragon that literally assailed her; and St. Marcel so led captive another by winding his stole round a dragon that ravaged the country round Paris. In one of the apocryphal Gospels the Apostle St. Philip is said to have met a dragon and to have spoken to him, " In the Name of the Lord Jesus go out of this place and depart into a desert apart where none of man come nigh thee."

In all these cases the original mystical idea has been lost in the lower and literal.

This same process can be found in other emblems, wrenched from their original and mystical meaning.

Nothing is more common in the Books of the Jews, the Acts of the Saints, and the writings of the early Fathers than comparisons taken from the lily and the rose, and of branches or staves that miraculously leafed or flowered. The flowers were considered mystically to represent the fragrance of holiness, and the sweetness of a Christian's soul; while the branch or staff in flower the type of purity. Thus, in one of the apocryphal writings it is stated a branch flowered in the hands of St. Joseph, designed for his espousals. This legend has been continually copied by painters, among others by Raphael, when he represents the marriage of the Blessed Virgin. The legend referred to shows how the apocryphal Gospel treated a mystical representation as a real fact, and shows exactly how the legend makers went along the same paths in their fabrications. They recounted, for instance, at the moment the grave of St. Salvius, Archbishop of Amiens, was opened a sweet odour stole forth and the ground around was immediately covered with flowers (Bollard, " Acta Sancta," tom. 7, ch. 3).

White roses growing indicated where the relics of St. Nicodemus were to be found (Plancy, " Dict. of Relics "). When the relics of St. Benoit were translated to Fleury the trees and the flowers broke forth into leaf and this legend is sculptured on the north door of the abbey of St. Benoit, while it is said the name of the village, formerly bearing another, was, to mark the miracle, changed into that of " Fleury." A real rose, the legend asserted, miraculously grew

Q

upon the grave of the boy St. William of Norwich
(Bolland, " Acta Sancta," xxv, p. 590).

Also after death a rose was found blossoming in the
hand of St. Antony of Stracona (Bolland, " Act.," xxi,
p. 365).   In the mouth of St. Benoist of Vallombrosa,
after long years from his death, a lily, as if just grown,
was found.   At his death a flower was discovered
similarly in the mouth of St. Louis of Toulouse
(Plancy, " Dict. of Relics ").

The vine, too, a representation of which, owing to
its mystical teaching, was used in the catacombs so
frequently by the early Christians, the legend makers,
not satisfied with its mystical teaching, introduced
into their saints' lives.   Thus it is woven into the
legend of St. Maximas of Nola, and into that of Urban
of Langres; following an eastern tradition, the vine of
Engaddi, they asserted, began to flourish forth at the
moment of Christ's birth.   Again, in their legend of
St. Panteleon, the martyr, when his head was cut off,
an olive branch was found attached to it—the head
itself full of flowers and fruit (Gantier, " Ribadeneira
Trad.," 27 July).

Perhaps one of the best illustrations of this
tendency in the legend makers and the people who
greedily believed their stories is that of St. Bonaventura and his Crucifix.   When St. Thomas
Aquinas asked of the saint where he obtained for his
writings their wonderful persuasive force and action,
Bonaventura pointed to the Crucifix which hung on
the wall, saying, " That it is that image which teaches
me all I say."   In vain worthy biographers of his life

said the saint meant it was only the Crucifix as an emblem of divine suffering which recalled to his mind all the mysteries of redemption, the legend came forth, and the credulous crowd believed, that this wooden cross spoke miraculously to him, and so Zurbaran, a Spanish painter, limned it on his canvas, though he attributed this fabulous miracle to another saint—Peter of Nola.

Another symbol, not so pleasant as flowers or palms, used to be sometimes placed in the hands of sculptured martyrs—their heads. The original purpose of this was to exemplify, as we popularly say, " they took their fate into their own hands," and courageously faced a martyr's death—but the mystical idea was soon, by the legend makers and the people, expanded into a real fact, that they miraculously carried their severed heads in their hands. It so occurs in the legendary life of St. Denis (Fleury, " Hist. Eccles.," bk. 17); in that of St. Firmin (" Legenda Aurea "); of St. Maurice (" Molanus de Hist. S. Maginum "); of St. Lucian; of St. Nicaise of Rheims (" Christlich Kunst Symbolik," p. 106), and many others.

There is also the strange aberration the legend makers suffered under—of, in their works, raising abstract virtues to the hierarchy of saints—thus Wisdom, Faith, Hope, and Charity were, in the Middle Ages, St. Sophia, St. Faith, St. Hope, and St. Charity. The church dedicated to Wisdom at Byzantium by Constantine was figuratively so named to commemorate the Divine Wisdom, but the legend makers and people soon humanized the mystery and pretended in that city St. Sophia possessed a real tomb,

" A la tombe Saincte Souphye
Ki fu virgene de bonne vie,"

as it appears in one of the legendary lays of the period.

Again, in seeking, by the intercession of some saint for the curing of some malady, so confused and ignorant were both legend makers and the people, that, from some fancied resemblance in the saint's name to their maladies, they made their petitions to such—and still do. Thus in France, St. Clare is invoked by those who suffer from their eyes because she enables people to see clearly (*clair*); St. Ouen cures deafness because he enables them to hear (*ouir*); St. Cloud cures boils (*clous*). Again, in certain parts of Germany St. Augustine is believed to rid people of diseases of the eye (*Auge*), and in others of a cough. There is one comparatively of recent date which enjoys a surprising and deplorable popularity. St. Expeditus has, owing to his name, been acclaimed the advocate of urgent causes!

As an instance of the gross materialistic view the commoner people and the ignorant mendicant friars took of the spiritual verities of the Christian faith may be mentioned a current idea in Germany of the heavenly state (translated by Sebastian Albui, p. 97): " Wine costs no more than a ' liard ' in the heavenly cellar, the angels there bake loaves and cakes at every one's command. Vegetables there of every sort spring up. Asparagus there is as big as a leg, and artichokes as big as a man's head. If it is a fast day (*un jour maigre*) the fish arrive there swimming, and St. Peter catches them with his bait and nets. St. Martha is there the cook, and St. Urban the cup-bearer." When these ideas were popular of the spiritual and heavenly state, can we wonder when the same materialistic legends of the images and histories of the popular saints in nearly every diocese were believed in by the people, that their higher and spiritual teaching was perfectly forgotten or misrepresented, and the grosser the legend the more it was current?

The truth is, in these later medievel ages the materialistic was overthrowing the mystical which the earlier of those ages so eminently possessed. An example of this can be seen in one of the charges brought against the Order of the Templars in Philip the Fair's reign. In their Initiation of Proselytes to the Order—from the earliest times—mysticism had obtained. Thus veiling the mysteries of the Holy Trinity, the candidate had three questions put to him. He had to ask three times for bread, water, and the fellowship of the Order. He made three vows. The knights observed three great fasts. They took the Sacrament three times a year. Alms were distributed three times a week. They ate meat on three days of the week only. On fast days they were allowed three dishes. They adored the Cross three times a year. Each swore in battle not to turn his back on three enemies. They flogged themselves three times in full Chapter of the Order. These mystical acts were brought against them in the age they were suppressed in, as evil and idolatrous, because in that age no more than they could see in the mystical figures besides the effigies of the Saints, anything else but a mundane and literal interpretation. (See " Instruction of the Inquisitor, William of Paris," Rayner, p. 4.)

Though the purpose of this paper has been chiefly to show how the mystical emblems of the saints were, by the legend weavers, interpreted in a materialistic manner, it might be as well to point out how, out of a great many instances, these same fertile brains, in order to embellish their legends, stultified history. History informs us that St. Procopius of Cæsarea belonged to the priesthood. Legend transformed him into an officer, and soon he was universally known under the title " Procopius dux."

Current legend describes Pope Xystus as dying on the Cross, yet we know for a fact from a letter of St. Cyprian, who was a contemporary, that Xystus died by the sword (Epist. lxxx).

Concerning St. Agnes there were current, as early as the fourth century, the most extraordinary reports, every one of which would probably be disproved by history, if history had not been wholly silent where she is concerned (" Franchi de Cavalieri S. Agnese nella tradizione, nella legenda," p. 28). Yet, in the legend makers' pages, she is most prominently described.

Take again the case of one of the less known St.

Margarets ("Acta Sancta," Oct.). This Margaret is said by the legend makers to have fled from her nuptial chamber disguised as a man. She hides herself in a monastery under the name of Pelagius. Accused of having seduced a nun, she suffers the penalty for a sin she could not have committed. Her innocence is only established after her death, when she received the name of St. Reparata!

Often, too, these Christian legend makers mix in them pagan ones. One instance is St. Lucian's legend, where there is the mixture of pagan and Christian material found by the persistence in which the number 15 occurs in connection with his name. The saint is said to have expired after 15 days of suffering. The fabulous dolphin in the legend brought his body to shore on the 15th day; he died after the Epiphany, which was the 15th of the month dedicated to the pagan Dionysus. And what is the meaning of the dolphin? It is one of the attributes of Dionysus. And why connected with St. Lucian? Because his feast coincided with St. Dionysus. Yet historically St. Lucian is one of the most authentic martyrs of the fourth century.

Again, there is the strange story by legend makers of a saint called Pelagia. There are three saints whose commemoration on the 8th of October in the Greek Church bear this name. Grouping together two or three saints of the same name, if they possessed two traditions which were not easy to reconcile, and reducing them into distinct persons was a common practice. This Pelagia originally seems to have been a girl of fifteen, who sees her father's house in the hands of ruthless soldiery: to escape them and preserve her virginity she flings herself from the roof of the house and dies. This dramatic episode was not enough for future legends—in them she is mixed up with Pelagia, a noted courtesan of Antioch, who was converted and a penitent and became a recluse.

This even was not sufficient. She was mixed with the pagan legends of Aphrodite, who wore the dress of a woman with the beard of a man (the worship of the Hemaphrodite). Yet the culture of her still remains in the Latin Church—the bearded woman has, by the influence of the legends, been raised to the altars. In Rome it is St. Falla (" Acta Sancta," Oct., vol. iii); in Span St. Paula, and in other places St. Liberata, or St. Wilgefortis and Ontkommer (*ibid.*, July, vol. v). The whole legend of this man-woman character of these saints being inspired by one of those veiled crucifixes of Christ, of which the " Volto Santo " of Lucca offers the best known example, and which the legends mistook for a veiled woman with a beard.

Now this paper is written with no sectarian bias. Its chief purport is to show, chiefly in the department of symbolism, how grossly in the later Middle Ages the symbolisms of the saints have been turned into material and untrustworthy events by the legend makers. It is such an extensive subject that it can only be touched on in this essay, yet, though written with no theological bias, it may be as well, as it is in the ancient Catholic Church images with their symbols still obtain and many legends are mixed up with those of an older and pagan cult, to mention on this subject what a learned priest of that Church, Father de la Haye, says in a book issued for Catholic priests and students of to-day, entitled " Legends of the Saints."

" We are far from denying the survival among Christian nations of a certain number of customs of which the origin is extremely remote, and which are in direct opposition to Christian beliefs and Christian ethics. The greater number of the superstitions against which the Church has perpetually made war, with changeful tactics and varying degrees of success, are an inheritance from our pagan ancestors. . . . It is an admitted fact that the larger collection of miracles bequeathed to us by the Middle Ages are compilations in which the most varied materials are mixed up at random, and which, in consequence, can only be used with the utmost circumspection. . . . There can be no doubt that a close study of their origin would lead to the identification of a number of pagan reminiscences and even formal adaptations."

We may add, these legends, if for religious romantic reading—despite their incertitude and fabrication—have a certain amount of historical value as showing the temperament of the people in those past ages; on the other hand, to found any spiritual teaching on them or dogma would be both dangerous and useless. Like the apocryphal Gospels, so quoted by our ancestors in the Middle Ages, they certainly, at the time, moulded religious thought; to us, in a more critical and unmystical age, who seek truth, even if,

in doing so, we destroy romance, in religion they fail.
In the words of that great saint (Augustine of Hippo):
" Religion should not be the product of our imagination.   Truth, under whatever form, is preferable to
anything which may be imagined."

GALAHAD OF THE HOLY GRAIL.
G. F. Watts, R.A.

By kind permission of Mr. F. Hollyer.

THE HOLY GRAIL

ALL stories that come down to us from past ages, if not based on known historical facts, are either (1) fabulous or (2) legendary. The fabulous are generally pagan; the legendary generally Christian; sometimes, as appears in this famous story of the Holy Grail, both fable and legend meet, and it is therefore extremely difficult to unravel their separate strands.

Now at the time this story of the Grail became world-wide in Western Europe, both fable and legend were avidly received. Paganism, or something very akin to it, despite the centuries past of Christianity, was still found, perhaps under a different name, active among the credulous, while the orthodox Faith, its primitive simplicity overgrown by un-historical legends, surrounded with false halos many whose deeds unwarranted such. As Matthew Arnold says: " The medieval story-teller pillaged an antiquity of which he did not fully possess the secret; he was like a peasant building his hut on the site of Halicarnassus, he built, but what he built was full of materials of which he knew not the history."

It is no wonder, therefore, that stories of a purely Celtic spirit of ancient and far-removed times changed their complexion as time went on. In such stories as Olwen and Rhonabwys' dream—as an instance of this development—Arthur is an indigenous British warrior, the air he breathes is purely Celtic, but later, as in Peredur and Geraint, Arthur and his followers have become Norman knights. For Norman chivalry and knight errantry have now become essential to popularize these Arthurian fables and legends. The great king still holds his court at Caerleon, but the adventures of his knights are bound up with customs they never knew, and dress and armour they never donned; even the locality they once moved in had become vague and misty. It was a part, indeed, of the price the story paid for its catholicity, that price paid to such as Geoffrey of Monmouth, Layamon, and other British and Anglo-Saxon historians or minstrels who transmitted it to the world outside the misty glens and mountains of Wales and the dolmen-spread fields of Brittany, which so long had hidden it.

The question therefore arises whether this Quest of the Holy Grail represents (1) a story entirely handed down from the dim past, or (2) whether it was a new invention at the time it became popular, or (3) whether the true explanation is it was a mixture of both these origins.

Now we find in both the earlier and later versions of the Grail there is a " Quest " set up; a quest by a certain person who, in the later versions, is a knight of Arthur's court. If we turn to the ancient Celts we find long before Christian times a folk-lore which may be called " The Great Fool Story," and a quest which has been found, in some shape or other, among nearly all people of the Aryan race. In it the heir is a boy, usually a young prince, born, or at least brought up, in a wilderness to escape the jealousy of his dead father's rival. In some versions his father was a great hero, in others a god, and signs and wonders have taken place at his birth. He is reared by his mother, but so dense is his understanding that he gains the name of The Fool. However, when of age, he is not too foolish for going on a great quest in search of his foes, nor too young but that he gains his purpose and slays many of both men and dragons, and with these trophies at last returns home. This story has been called also " The Aryan Expulsion and Return." It is found embodied in eight fabulous stories in Celtic literature alone. Here there is certainly a strong likeness to the after and celebrated quest of the Grail by a young warrior.

Again, there exist in both Irish and Gaelic and Breton folk-lore many references to a talismanic spear—generally dripping with blood, also a cup or cauldron, the spear representing the power of destruction, the cup the powers of healing, wherein whatever is dead and thrown in revives. In the later story of the Grail, the spear and the holy cup (Grail) appear. Again, in the Arthurian fable or legend there is prominently brought forward the sickness unto death from a wound received, of a prince called " The Fisher-King," and till he is restored to health and rescued from death all the adjacent country remains arid and unfertile.

If we turn to the Aryan myths of Greece in their cult of Atys or Adonis we find similar traits. When Adonis is strong, virile, and alive, the land is fertile, when he, for a time, succumbs to his wound and dies, the outward world dies also. In both these remote fables of the Celts and the Greeks, the idea of fertility depending on a higher power, being in its prime or decay, appears. As a French writer puts it: " En réalité c'est sur la conception de la vie physique consiclerée dans son origene et dans son action et dans le double principe qui l'anime que repose tout le cycle religieuse des peuples orientaux et de l'antiquité."

There can be found also other curious parallels in the Celtic and Grecian Myths. During the days of mourning for the death of the god Adonis, women cut off their hair—they also wept plentifully. In the Grail story where the Fisher-king lies wounded to death, twelve maidens stand outside weeping bitterly. In the Percival version of the Quest another maiden appears who has cut off all her hair for the same reason of mourning.

Again there existed in the earliest versions of the Grail mysterious allusions to certain objects, either pagan or Christian. Now, if Christian, we should find these said objects treated as such in these earliest as well as in the later ones we possess. But such is not the case. In " Sir Percival " there is no mention whatever of sword, lance, spear, cup, or dish. In the ancient Welsh Cèltic series of tales, the Mabinogi—a bleeding spear and a salver containing a man's head—are introduced, but with no hint of their being relics of Christ's passion. In Wolfram's version of the Grail the contents of the salver are still essentially earthly—a hundred pages take from before the mysterious Grail white napkins containing bread, and from it come food and drink for all who sit feasting at no spiritual banquet. In another variant of Wolfram's version the Grail is a precious stone yielding plenteous store of meat and drink to all. There is no doubt, therefore, these objects, originally far from a Christian source, were representations of some ancient Druidical usages and their knowledge long kept alive through Celtic tradition.

For a long time, therefore, it seems no evidence for any Christian symbolical meaning attached to the Grail. And from the whole phase of it in its earliest form, there is no doubt it had a Celtic and pagan origin—founded on the common Aryan religion, typified also in the Greek story of Adonis, of the Sun worship, and of the seasons, of the withdrawal that is of the sun in winter typified by the wounded Fisher-king—of his restoration, and so also of Adonis in the spring when all the earth breaks out into fertility; while the " objects " or implements—the spear, the cauldron, or precious stone—were the objects of some far-off ritual used in worship of the same solar deity. Indeed, lance and cup were in truth connected together in a symbolic relation long ages before the institution of Christianity. They were sex symbols, and so their use in the worship of the sun, the primal giver of fertility. The lance or spear represented the male, the cup or vase the female reproductive energy (see Dulaure, " Des Divinites Generatances," p. 77).

Now these ancient traditional fables or legends were revived by the Welsh bards during the Norman invasion of their country. Sensible of their antiquity and mystery, and not too careful to offer an explanation of their meaning, with their countrymen beaten down on every side, they consoled themselves, as Celts, by living in a more glorious pass wherein these traditions had their rise. The story of the Great

Fool, being sung by them as one who suffered contumely and yet was in the end victorious, heartened up their beaten hearers, while the mystical Arthur, in like manner, was evoked from the past with greater power than ever to show the world what a British prince and a Celtic nation could achieve if they would.

Now in approaching the Christian version, as now received, of this story of the Holy Grail, when it was first taken up by the compilers, or, rather, transmuters of the original old Celtic tradition, we must not expect that any one leading idea was kept always in view. In many cases mere invention of new material seems to be all that those compilers thought of. To regard the series of legends as a whole, and to find that they always embody some central thought is just what, as Skeat says in his " Joseph of Arimathea," we moderns are so prone to do, but it may be doubted whether the writers of them would not be astonished at such a proceeding.

A matter greatly disputed up to the present day is who first transformed a Celtic folk story into a Christian legend or allegory?

The most probable is, that some Norman-English monk, during the time of interest in Welsh affairs under Henry II, introduced the story to the French-reading world in a version which we do not now possess. That between 1170 and 1190 Robert de Borron took it further, and contemporaneously with him (1189) Chrestien de Troyes began his " Li Contes del Grael," the main source of which was the third part of Borron's poem—while about 1225 Percival le Gallois compiled his own from all previous versions, including both Borron's and Chrestien's. But if we thus among other competitors for this Christianized legend give the initial place to Chrestien, there is the strongest possible evidence that Chrestien himself admits he was not inventing the main facts, but re-telling an already known folk story (see Weston's "From Ritual to Romance," p. 180).

The time Borron and Chrestien wrote was a time peculiarly fitted to receive this legend of the Grail, and so the story of Arthur and his Knights of the Round Table was accepted with especial readiness. The stories of Charlemagne and Alexander, and the sagas of Teutonic tribes, with the tale of Imperial Rome itself, though still affording subject matter to the wandering *jongleur* and monkish annalist, paled before the fame of the British King. The instinct which led the twelfth and thirteenth centuries thus to place the Arthurian story above all others was that it fell in with their spirit of romance, for those were pre-eminently the ages of the romantic temper. Again, there was nothing, too, in them to disturb the existing Norman Conqueror in England, France, and Sicily. They were charmed rather by their tender melancholy. "It is by this trait of idealism and universality," writes M. Renan, "that the story of Arthur won such astonishing vogue throughout the whole world." From the close connection of Wales with Brittany, and Brittany contiguous to France, and Wales to England, the body of this Arthurian romance was carried by these two powerful nations all over Western Europe—until it was sung on every troubadour's and *trouvère's* harp, and told in every castle hall.

R

Then another element helped its spread. The great excitement of the middle of the twelfth century was the second Crusade, begun in 1146, while a little earlier the Order of the Knights Templars had been established, their object religious glory, their destination the East. How exactly all this reproduced the history of Arthur and his knights seeking a holy object in the quest of the Holy Grail and finding it likewise in the East! It has been said that Chrestien de Troyes meant to portray, when he took in hand to re-model the Grail to a Christian idea, the knight Percival as the hero—if so he failed; no better morality he gave him than that rife at his period, nothing in his quest spiritual—simply knight errantry; it therefore needed Borron and those that followed him to give us this perfect knight without shame and reproach—young Galahad—the finder of the Holy Grail, and to embody in him chasteness in all he did, and by him to teach that only by passing into a land intermediary between earth and heaven, is the quest achieved.

Perhaps it was owing to this ideal in knighthood of perfect chasteness, bravery, and yet perfect innocence, that the story of the Grail " caught on " with those who heard it.

It was a revelation, new and needed as such— " Love-service " was then everywhere practised in that age of chivalry wherever knights drew swords and women were fair and frail. It was therefore a new conception brought to the courts of Europe that a young knight could be as chaste as a child, self-denying as an anchorite, and yet brave as the bravest. From dim-clouded Camelot to Provence, from

Provence to Jerusalem, this story spread, and everywhere roused enthusiasm.

It therefore was a favourable period when the story of the Quest appeared.

(2) The " implements "—the lance, the spear, the cup—found in its ancient Celtic traditional story required little to turn such to Christian ones. The extraordinary fraud which gave out that the Holy Lance which pierced the Saviour's side had been found at the Siege of Antioch in 1098 was still remembered and treasured as an article of belief by every Crusader. To turn the spear of Celtic myth, which had pierced the Fisher-king, into this Holy Lance that had pierced the Saviour, was easily done. The mysterious " Grail-Ark," too, in which so many wonders in the pagan version of the story was seen, was again easily turned into the Holy Sepulchre, the aim of the Crusaders.

Skeat quotes a passage in the Anglo-Saxon version of the legend of St. Veronica edited by Godwin, for the Cambridge Antiquaries Society. In it Joseph says of himself: " I was one of those who guarded His Sepulchre and bent my head and thought to see Him, but I beheld nothing of Him, but I saw two angels, one at the head and the other at the foot."

The Druid cauldron or dish was easily turned into the mysterious Grail itself; it only required some clever manipulation to associate it with the legendary Arthur and his paladins. This was found in the ancient tradition that at Glastonbury that king lay buried in a sleep which one day, like Barbarossa's, should be ended when his countrymen's needs called him, while Glastonbury had this in its favour—the tradition that Joseph of Arimathea there first came to preach the Gospel to the heathen Celts. It seems to the writer, however, an afterthought, and arising from the necessity of some reason being given for turning the pagan cauldron or dish into the chalice or cup of the Christian legend, to make Joseph the first who introduced the Grail. It was obvious to the transformers of the legend if its Christian form was to be held, no better person could be found than Joseph. The evangels had recorded how it was he that took and prepared for burial his Saviour; might he not have preserved in some cup a few drops of the sacred Blood? At all events, it was in Joseph the Christianized form of the cup became incorporated. And it was he who handed it on to his kin who became, as Arthur did, princes in the land, till, in the words of him who dwelt by the Western Seas (Hawker) himself:

> " Evil days came on
> And evil men; the garbage of their sin
> Tainted the land, and all things holy fled,
> The Sangrael was not! "

The series indeed of the Grail seems to have begun with the story of Joseph, as seen from above, because he was the great British saint and was said to have been buried at Glastonbury where Arthur, too, lay. Hence the idea of introducing the story of Arthur in a romance concerning Joseph arose naturally enough.

Again, this disappearance of the Grail, the reader can see, was necessary for the sake of its after quest. There could have been no quest if it had remained at Glastonbury, so we find the absence of it when we go through the list of the relics of Glastonbury as given in the " Monasticon " (vol. i, p. 5). And surely this Holy Grail or Cup, if materialized, would have had a place of honour where, among other far stranger relics, we find recorded in this same " Monasticon " : " Some pieces of the Bread of the Five Loaves," " Some of the Gold the Wise Men offered," " Some of our Lord's Hair," " Some of the Virgin's Milk " (a very favourite relic in these ages of superstition), " Two Teeth of St. Peter," etc., at Glastonbury.

It was, thank God, to a finer and more spiritual atmosphere Borron, and those who followed him in transmuting from a pagan Celtic to a Christian legend, removed the Holy Grail or Cup in which our Lord's Blood was once gathered.

That Grail or Cup was evanescent. It was seen only at times, and then in the hands of flying angels. It was visible and then invisible. It shone as the sun, and then the clouds of earth and sin hid it from mortal sight.

> " Then of a summer night it came to pass
> While the great banquet lay along the hall,
> That Galahad would sit down in Merlin's chair,
> And all at once as there we sat, we heard
> A cracking and a riving of the roofs
> And rending, and a blast, and overhead
> Thunder, and in the thunder was a cry,
> And in the blast there smote along the hall
> A beam of light seven times more clear than day,
> And down the long beam stole the Holy Grail
> All overcovered with a luminous cloud,
> . . . and every knight beheld his fellow's face
> As in a glory."

So in the legend of the Grail when Christianized, there is nothing tangible—nothing gross—a great mystery, and so most artistic, nay more, far more spiritual than if men's hands could have touched and handled that holy thing.

It was for a later age, never satisfied unless it could embody what was of the spirit, in the sordidness of actual touch, that this Holy Grail was said to be handled and imprisoned in a storehouse of similar relics.

These later legends inform us that it was finally transported to India, and still remains there. However, at the capture of Cesarea in 1101 the Crusaders found what they thought was the Grail in the form of a dish made out of one great emerald (Roquefort, *s.v.* Graal). This is absurd on the face of it—for if there was, which is most unlikely, a dish or cup used by our Lord and His poor fisherfolk at the Last Supper, a dish made out of costly emerald would have been impossible for such.

This story goes on to say it was afterwards sent to Genoa and there shown as a relic till Napoleon I transported it to Paris. In 1815 it was sent back to Genoa, but was cracked in its transit. It can still be seen in the treasury of the church of San Lorenzo. It is really made of greenish glass. Another legend says that one (a Grail) was sent to England to Henry III by the patriarch of Jerusalem, and also that another once existed at Constantinople. The old book of Melkin tells us that Joseph did not bring a dish to England at all, but two cruets, which were buried with him, and will be found when his burial place is discovered.

These variant and conflicting traditions prove that

no tangible Grail ever existed outside the original poetic legend, and that if then found it was only of the spiritual world.

And for this reason the legend of this Holy Grail still possesses a strange and tender allurement. Though the troubadour and *trouvère* and the Welsh bards who once sung of it are, with knights who tilted and the fair ones whose favours they wore, long time dust, its quest is still never over while man's soul seeks something beyond the finite that surrounds him, and sees a flash—like the flash of the Holy Grail in a riven sky, that gives for a moment a lifting of death's dark veil. And so, too, of Galahad, of him who goes the quest, to him clad in shining harness— young, brave, living in the world though above it— to him, and not to an anæmic saint or mystical votaress—but to a lad strong and in the world, it shows that if only a man possesses good faith and a life of chastity, the unseen things of God become seen; that though no monk's robe but a corselet covers the heart, if the heart is pure it finds its Grail.

The meaning of the word " Grail " or " Graal " has been the subject of much discussion. The most probable is, it is from the low Latin " Gradale " from a diminutive " cratella," a " mixing bowl," which was used at great feasts (Roquefort). Another interpretation of " San Graal," the two words having lost their original meaning, is, they meant " sang real "—real blood. But " sang real " does not mean " real blood," if anything it means " blood royal." In this sense it might be applied to the Holy Blood in the cup being that of the Son of David.

To sum up this paper:

(1) It has been shown that the original source of this legend was Celtic and pagan. That it shared in common with other Aryan myths the worship of the Sun God, whether directly so, or as in the Greek mythology under that of Adonis or Atys. That in this legend in its earliest form is to be found the same idea of fertility being caused by the shining or reverse (wounding) and disappearance of the solar deity and the changes of the seasons from fertility to the reverse.

(2) It has further been shown its transformation into a Christian and beautiful legend or allegory, being chivalric, fitted it to the time in which it spread through Europe—that of the Crusades.

(3) Again, as many took it up to alter or add to it, it is extremely difficult, if not impossible, at the present day, to say, for the Christian version we now have, who were its authors. In this paper, from out of many competitors, the writer has preferred Chrestien de Troyes and Borron, both afterwards amalgamated in his own version by Percival le Gallois. And really, except in an antiquarian light, it matters little who compiled, altered, or added to this beautiful legend of the Holy Grail. What matters it to one beholding a beautiful statue whence its marble was hewn, or drinking in the loveliness of some old painter from where his canvas was obtained? So of this legend —while we possess this charming legend full of rich allegory, its original source is a secondary matter.